The Publisher gratefully acknowledges the support of

EssEl WORLD
Recharge your emotions

WATER KINGDOM
ASIA'S LARGEST THEME WATER PARK

Birds
OF MUMBAI

SUNJOY MONGA

Illustrations
CARL D'SILVA

IBH

INDIA BOOK HOUSE

CONTENTS

INTRODUCTION

There's a flutter of shadows in downtown Mumbai's Nariman Point as a flock of pigeons dashes in a frenzy. A predictable scene in the city, one would imagine. But wait, there's more to it. Tearing through the pigeons is an adult Peregrine Falcon. A fleeting glimpse is all that the streamlined hunter allows, as it swerves swiftly into the jungle of skyscrapers. Perhaps the falcon managed an evening strike. If not, it will carry on with its formidable attack the next morning; perhaps even in neighbouring Cuffe Parade or around the Gothic splendour of the University Clock Tower.

   Meanwhile, as rush-hour traffic hurtles past in this hectic business district, a Tailorbird calls animatedly from a flush of leafy exotics, joined by the cheerful whistles of a Redvented Bulbul pair. The rotting branch of a roadside Gulmohur tree offers refuge to a Coppersmith Barbet that has dug its nest-cavity over hawkers and passers-by. A couple of hundred feet above the busy street, a motley crowd of swallows and a few House Swifts dash about, hawking tiny insects over India's corporate heart. Along the famed Marine Drive, on the seaside ooze and rock in the evening low-tide, a couple of solemn and serene Reef Egrets loom over a bevy of other active waders. A smattering of gulls from the Himalaya, Central Asia and the Arctic Tundra, floats low over Mumbai's waterfronts.

   On India's western seafront, Mumbai city embraces a glorious wealth of biodiversity. Located at the northern tip

House Crow – the most visible symbol of Mumbai's bird life..

Exotic garden plants are an ideal resource for the industrious Tailorbird.

of the Malabar Coast, its unique bio-geographic features and moist climate have spawned a variety of habitats. The region is blessed with an abundance of birds – over a quarter of India's bird species have been observed here. Like Mumbai's human residents, its birds too are a cosmopolitan hodgepodge that include a sprinkling from the neighbouring Sahyadri Mountains.

An economic powerhouse with a burgeoning population of over 13 million people, the city's history is one of steady development and urbanization. Nearly sixty years ago, the late Dr Salim Ali and Humayun Abdulai wrote about the birds of Mumbai in the context of a feverish spurt of urbanising activity: "Where but a few years since the call of curlews, oyster-catchers and sandpipers resounded at low tide through the stillness of night, the hooting of motor horns and the incessant din of scurrying traffic now proclaim Ballard Estate as one of the city's liveliest business centres".

It seems miraculous that so many birds survive the deteriorating habitats, fearsome noise, pollution and general apathy of one of this planet's most densely-populated urban areas. While some bird populations in the region are decreasing, others appear to thrive like never before, with a few even staging an encouraging comeback.

Climate and topography affect every region's biodiversity – and Mumbai is wondrously blessed on both counts. The climate is moderately warm with copious rainfall; and there are many distinct habitats. The region's avifauna is almost uniformly divided (in terms of species range) between wetland, forest, and grass and scrub species.

Wetland habitats dominate the region's western length. Ranging from sandy and rocky beaches to impenetrable mangrove creeks, tidal mudflats and a mix of marshy lands, lakes and reservoirs, these wetlands sometimes play host to enormous bird congregations, as seen along Thane Creek, Uran and Sewri Bay.

Forests as well as grass and scrub dominate the populous Konkan strip between the coast and the Sahyadri. This verdant area is contiguous with forested tracts towards the north, with hill-ranges to the northeast and south of the island city. Though largely disjunct from the Sahyadri, the composition and variety of bird species in the region is greatly enriched by these mountains.

Interestingly, all protected sites here are forest areas. The Sanjay Gandhi National Park, spread over Mumbai and Thane municipal limits, is the largest natural forest contained by a metropolis.

Like elsewhere in the country, here too, an increasing number of bird species are being seen at the edges of specific habitats. This mix of tree-dotted cultivation, groves and fallow lands has increased considerably in the Konkan and along hill-slopes, usually at the cost of original habitat.

The urban areas of this region comprise the municipal limits of Mumbai, Thane, Navi Mumbai, Kalyan–Dombivli. The human hand has, often unintentionally, introduced

The region's forests are home to vivid songsters like the Orange-headed Thrush.

conditions beneficial to many bird species. A profusion of flowering, fruiting trees, parks and gardens, landfill sites overflowing with refuse and derelict patches of green provide a vast variety of habitats. Nearly 150 species of birds have been sighted within this urban realm.

The post-monsoon period marks the beginning of the finest birding period, with the arrival of masses of wintering birds. Several are Passage Migrants, halting for a few hours or a few days, while others are Local Migrants, from the bordering Sahyadri and Deccan Plateau.

Birds are often considered a vital indicator of a region's eco-health. Studies in some parts of the world have revealed that not only are an increasing number of birds

adapting to urban areas, surrounding farmlands and groves but also bird-densities are sometimes higher here than in protected woodlands. It has been quite the same in the Mumbai region. While a phenomenal rise in numbers of such commensals as House Crow and Rock Pigeon have been observed in recent years, this period has also witnessed an alarming drop in numbers of several other species in urban areas as well as adjoining forests.

It is hoped that more people are drawn to the region's birds and environment, to cherish the arrival of thousands of flamingos at Sewri Bay, the flash of Kingfisher blue and the fluted notes of a Golden Oriole.

The nesting Black-throated Weaver – a captivating discovery for the region.

Watching birds is a pretty simple, generally inexpensive and utterly relaxing pastime. Getting accustomed to it is like learning how to drive a car. At first it appears difficult, with so many actions to be performed and amid all manners of obstacles! But things soon fall into place. Just like changing gears, adjusting speed, keeping track of the traffic around become routine actions, so it is with watching birds.

While an important prerequisite to birding is that you must go out, you do not necessarily have to take off into some remote wilderness. It is often possible to quite easily observe many birds around where you live and work.

The art of birding is based on certain clues and hints. Let's look at it this way: Assume you can recognise a parrot, owl, peafowl, crow and pigeon. You're already on step one – Observation. Now, when you do see some bird, something tells you it isn't any of the five birds you know. Perhaps it is the colour, or size, appearance, some behaviour that is 'different'. This is step two – Elimination.

Although your first few bird-watching trips can be 'casual' affairs, it is best if you accompany regular birders. You could also read a bit about the area you plan to visit. Investing in a pair of binoculars would be a great idea too. Silence, and comfortable, inconspicuous clothing will win you rich rewards when bird-watching.

Some field pointers that will help you on any bird-watching venture:

Size: Do familiarize yourself with sizes of commonly seen birds. This way, new birds can be put in a 'size bracket' – an important pointer to recognizing the bird.

Colour: The myriad colours of birds are not just a joy to see, but serve as great pointers for identification. It pays to be 'tuned in' to colour tones, shades, etc.

Shape: You will soon be able to recognize a bird merely by its silhouette. With experience, the shape and form of a bird begins to tell a lot. A mix of attributes such as posture, build, head-shape, define a bird. Learning to recognize a bird by its shape would be a giant step forward in your bird-watching voyage.

Other field-marks: Many birds have peculiar markings which help distinguish between species, even between sexes. These can take the form of streaks and barrings, crown-stripes, supercilium (eye-brows), eye-stripes, wing-bars, tail-bands; or physical modifications of feathers into crests, decorative plumes or peculiarly shaped tails.

Behaviour: Just like every individual has a certain personality, a certain temperament, so does every group of birds; sometimes even species of bird have distinctive demeanours. This is another attribute that helps tremendously in birding. It's like your ability to recognize someone familiar from a distance even though you cannot see the details of their features. Just the posture or style of walking tells you it is someone you know.

Flight: Birds are best known for flight. The greater majority of birds fly and many have characteristic flight. The way a bird flies reveals a lot about itself.

Habitat preference: Birds prefer specific types of habitats and usually keep to these. Within a habitat itself, birds choose from the forest floor and low bush to the middle level and high canopy. Free as a bird might seem, the fact is that the greater majority of feathered folk live in nature's unseen yet highly organised 'cages' where maintaining and defending territories is key to survival. Once you are broadly aware of what to expect in any particular habitat, your bird-watching activity acquires a specific focus.

Calls: Many birds have melodious voices unparalleled in the living world. Most have an individuality when it comes to voice and you will soon be able to identify birds without even seeing them. In fact, expert bird-watchers often rely as much on ears as eyes, sometimes even more on ears to locate and identify birds.

After a few bird-watching sallies you'll be amazed at how comfortably and quickly things fall into place. There couldn't be a more rewarding couple of hours than in the company of birds. Moreover, bird-watching can be your stepping stone to experiencing nature's other wonders and to environmental issues at large.

You could begin right in your Mumbai backyard, neighbourhood park, tree-lined avenue or rocky coast, perhaps even on your morning walk.

Happy birding!

BABBLERS Large, varied family of small and medium-size, mostly brownish birds of scrub, middle-storey of forest, where, many rummage; highly vocal, some with diagnostic calls; weak fliers, flying low.

BARBETS Arboreal, stocky birds; largely greenish, difficult to sight; diagnostic calls; largely frugivorous.

BEE-EATERS Slender-built, predominantly greenish birds; slender, slightly down-curved beak; hawk winged-insects; dig nest-cavities in mud-walls.

BULBULS Medium-size, generally dull-plumaged; active and perky; insectivorous and frugivorous; cheerful, whistling call-notes.

BUNTINGS Small, largely terrestrial birds, sometimes with larks, finches and sparrows, gleaning seeds on ground; males often more brightly plumaged; some can be gregarious during winter.

BUTTONQUAILS Small, skulking quail-like ground-birds of damp, open areas; polyandrous, females larger, more colourful; males incubate; differ from quails in having three toes; feed on grain, shoots, small insects.

CHATS, ROBINS & THRUSHES Large group ranging from sparrow-size redstarts to pigeon-size thrushes; longish-legged, terrestrial living; hop on ground, rummaging amid leaf-litter; also settle in trees, bush; diagnostic call-notes of many; some very richly voiced.

CORMORANTS Dark-plumaged, usually gregarious waterbirds; excellent swimmers and divers; when swimming only head may be visible; strong, straight flight, neck held out; bask with wings out-stretched; largely fish-eaters; may feed on tadpoles, crustaceans.

CROWS & TREEPIES Large, strong-flying birds; crows chiefly black; gregarious and noisy; omnivorous; treepies more colourful, longer-tailed with distinctive calls.

CUCKOOS Slender, usually arboreal, long-tailed; difficult to locate; diagnostic calls. **Parasitic Cuckoos**, incl Hawk-cuckoos, lay eggs in nests of other birds. Non-hawk-cuckoos have long, narrower wings. Feed on insects, fruit, seldom flower nectar. **Non-Parasitic Cuckoos** include Malkohas, Coucal. The former are very long-tailed and broad-winged. Coucals have weak flight, deep, booming calls; wide, varied diet.

CUCKOOSHRIKE & MINIVETS **Cuckooshrikes** are medium-size, largely grayish, arboreal and insectivorous; many quite rich of voice. **Minivets** are brightly coloured (scarlet in males, yellower in females); arboreal, insectivorous; slender-built, long-tailed.

CURLEWS, GODWITS & SANDPIPERS Long-legged waders with long, slender beak; shades of brown, grey-brown, with whitish undersides; wing, tail marks often important identification clues; several have diagnostic calls; can be highly gregarious; curlews, whimbrels have distinctly down-curved beak; **snipes** have very long beak; godwits are very long-legged with long beak.

DRONGOS Slender, black birds with long, forked, sometimes peculiarly developed, tails; chiefly arboreal; may descend into bush; highly vocal; chiefly insectivorous, hunting on wing; also visit flowering trees.

DUCKS Typically gregarious, chunky-bodied. Includes geese, surface-feeding (dabbling) and diving ducks. Feed on grain, shoots of crops, aquatic insects; fast, strong flight, neck out-stretched. **Surface-feeding (dabbling) ducks** prefer vegetation-covered ponds/marshes; often up-end (head immersed, tail projecting out of water) or dabble on marshy ground; rise directly from water; most have bright-coloured speculum; includes Gadwall, Garganey, Mallard, Pintail, Shoveller, Wigeon, Common teal. **Diving ducks** prefer open waters; some may roost on sea; dive for food; require some pattering or running along water surface before taking off. Includes Pochards.

FANTAIL *See* FLYCATCHERS.

FLAMINGOS Highly gregarious, tall, aquatic birds; very long legs and neck stretched out in flight; peculiar feeding style, long neck bent and beak immersed; feed on minute marine life (on which specially adapted to feed), crustaceans and molluscs.

FLOWERPECKERS Tiny, fidgety, arboreal birds; short, thick beak and stumpy tail; feed on fruits, berries, including of certain epiphytic plants; also insects, small spiders; call-notes surprisingly loud for size.

FLYCATCHERS Small birds of forest, groves; insectivorous, making short aerial sallies; seldom many together; often amid mixed bird parties; males of many species brightly coloured; harsh, grating call-notes; short song in some.

FRANCOLIN *See* PARTRIDGES & PHEASANTS

GREBES Duck-like, aquatic birds with pointed beak, almost tail-less shape; excellent swimmers, divers; feed on aquatic insects, small frogs, crustaceans.

GULLS & TERNS Buoyant, often gregarious, pale-grey and white waterside birds; dark heads in several species when breeding. **Gulls** are medium to large, with broader wings, webbed feet; surface feeders, often settle on water; many scavenge. **Terns** are slender-built; narrower, pointed wings, long, pointed beak, tail forked in several species; acrobatic flight; capture fish by diving into water.

HERONS, EGRETS & BITTERNS Long-legged wading birds with pointed beak; some are squat with proportionately shorter neck, legs; several have decorative plumes when breeding (Apr-Aug); head and long neck tucked in during (leisurely) flight; often remain motionless for long; some are nocturnal and/or crepuscular. Feed on fish, frogs, aquatic insects and crustaceans; many species breed in mixed heronries on large trees here.

HOOPOE Slender-built, crested bird with diagnostic black and white wings; feeds almost entirely on ground.

HORNBILLS Large to very large, with diagnostic huge, de-curving, horn-like beak; peculiar nesting habits, female sealed in tree-cavity; male feeds from outside; feed on fruits, insects, lizards, frogs.

IORAS Bright coloured, richly-voiced, arboreal birds; largely insectivorous; often in mixed bird parties. **Iora** is sparrow-size, greenish-yellow and black. **Leafbirds** are bulbul-size, greenish, excellent mimics.

JACANAS Marsh birds with unusually long legs, toes; walk on surface vegetation; distinctive piping calls; polyandrous.

KINGFISHERS Vividly coloured with long, pointed beak; most feed on fish; dig long tunnel-nest in mud-walls; diagnostic call-notes of several species.

LAPWINGS *See* PLOVERS

LARKS Drab-plumaged terrestrial birds; run briskly on ground; field identification of several species not very easy; most have rich, melodious flight song.

LEAFBIRDS *See* IORAS

MARTINS *See* SWALLOWS

MYNAS & STARLINGS Widespread group of medium-sized birds; some seen in habitation; active, noisy; wide food preference.

NIGHTJARS Highly cryptic-plumaged, nocturnal birds; long tail, wings; short beak with wide gape; hawk insects in flight; spend day on ground or settled lengthwise along branch; at night may be seen in vehicle head-light beam on roads, paths; diagnostic calls.

ORIOLES Myna-size, arboreal birds; males more brightly coloured; feed on insects, fruits, flower nectar; harsh, grating notes and mellow whistling notes.

OWLS Soft-plumaged birds of distinctive appearance; roundish head, large, forward-facing eyes, facial disc and short tail; some have ear-tufts; rarely sighted during day, when well hidden in foliage, cavities, house lofts, other dark sites; many have diagnostic calls; all are predatory; diet consists of insects, lizards, rodents, small birds.

OYSTERCATCHER Large coastal wader with pied plumage; feeds on molluscs, crustaceans.

PAINTED SNIPE Secretive bird of marsh-edge; crepuscular and nocturnal; polyandrous, female more colourful.

PARAKEETS Long-tailed, green birds; reddish, hooked beak; distinctive, shrill screams, often in fast, direct flight; chiefly arboreal, frugivorous; also raid standing crop, orchards; sometimes large flocks. Vernal Hanging Parakeet is an agile, acrobatic bird; stub-tailed.

PARTRIDGES & PHEASANTS Secretive, terrestrial birds of dense cover; many beautifully patterned but difficult to observe; most exhibit sexual dimorphism; diagnostic call-notes; emerge in clearings, paths to feed on seeds, grain, shoots, insects, worms; run into cover on disturbance; tight-sitters, taking flight as last resort.
  Quails are very small; roundish build, short-tail.
  Francolins & Spurfowl are smaller than domestic fowl; some may roost in trees.
  Pheasants (Grey Junglefowl, Peafowl) are large, showy birds; long, highly developed tail; males can be very colourful and flashy.

PETRONIA *See* SPARROW

PIGEONS & DOVES Strong-flying, chubby, small-headed; several are gregarious; seed and/or fruit-eaters; some strictly arboreal, others scrub-dwelling; also glean on ground; most have diagnostic call-notes.

PIPITS *See* WAGTAILS

PITTAS Stout-looking, short-tailed; bright-coloured but secretive; hop much on ground, sometimes flying into trees; distinctive whistling notes.

PLOVERS Sandy-plumaged waders; shorter, thicker beak, thickish neck; several lapwings have brightly coloured facial wattles. Many are gregarious; run in short spurts, body bent slantingly forward to pick food.

QUAILS *See* PARTRIDGES & PHEASANTS

RAILS & CRAKES Short-tailed, secretive, birds of marsh-edge cover; upright bearing, head often jerked while walking; flight short and weak, legs dangling awkwardly; most vocal in overcast weather; feed on seeds, shoots of aquatic plants, insects, mollusks.

RAPTORS Medium to large-size predatory (or scavenging) birds; powerful, hooked beak and sharp talons;

dominant colours shades of brown, grey and white, with diagnostic bands, bars, streaks or stripes in plumage. **Kites** prefer open country; have longish, angular wings; floating (buoyant) flight, gliding often. **Hawks** are arboreal, usually solitary; prefer forest, tree-dotted cultivation, groves; small or medium-size, with roundish wings, long tail; unfeathered, longish yellow legs; several have distinctive whistling screams; fly amongst trees to flush out small birds. **Harriers** are slender-built birds of open country, marsh-side; glide low, with few wing-beats. **Buzzards** are broad-winged birds of open country; soar and circle high regularly. **Eagles** are a highly varied group of large raptors; long, often broad wings; seen in a variety of habitats, including wetlands and coast; powerful flight, soaring high; most are hunters but several also scavenge. **Osprey** is a waterside, fish-eating raptor with long wings. **Vultures** are large, scavenging birds; have naked part of neck; numbers drastically fallen in recent years. **Falcons** are small to medium-size raptors with pointed, long wings; fast flight, with rapid wing-beats; many hunt in air or stoop at great speed.

ROLLER   Stocky-looking, big-headed bird of open country; often sighted along road and rail journeys, settled on exposed perches; brightly coloured wings in flight.

SHRIKES   Medium-sized, big-headed, long-tailed birds; upright stance; hooked beak; most have broad black band through eyes; pounce on prey (insects, small lizards, rodents); harsh screaming calls; seldom fly into high branches.

SNIPES   *See* CURLEWS, GODWITS & SANDPIPERS

SPARROW   *See* WEAVERS, MUNIAS & FINCHES

STILTS & AVOCETS   Lanky waders with pied plumage; very long legs, beak straight (**Stilt**) or peculiarly up-curved (**Avocet**); usually gregarious; often wade into deep water.

STORKS, SPOONBILLS & IBISES   **Storks** are very large birds with long legs and neck; large, heavy beak. Often soar high on thermals; slow, unhurried flight; feed on fish, frogs, crustaceans. **Spoonbills & Ibises** are gregarious, with diagnostic beak; long and down-curved in ibises, flattened in spoonbill; legs and neck outstretched in flight; mostly inland marshes, occasionally coastal tracts.

SUNBIRDS   Small, restless birds of bush and/or canopy; males brilliantly coloured long, slender, pointed beak suited for nectar-feeding; also hunt out insects, spiders.

SWALLOWS   Slender-built birds with pointed wings; mostly on wing, hawking insects; perch on overhead wires, rock-ledges; many often around water; **Swallows** steel-blue and white, with bright chestnut; long, forked tail in many; often highly gregarious. **Martins** chiefly grey-brown or blackish in colour.

SWIFTS Drab-coloured, usually seen in flight; long, scythe-like wings; tail forked or short, square-ended; most settle only on nest, or to collect wet-mud/water on ground, when rising with some difficulty.

TITS Small, active birds; inquisitive and noisy; often in mixed bird parties; arboreal, may descend low.

THRUSHES *See* CHATS, ROBINS & THRUSHES

TREEPIES *See* CROWS & TREEPIES

TROGON Broad-winged, long-tailed; arboreal, hawk insects from perch.

TURNSTONE *See* PLOVERS

WAGTAILS Slender-built, terrestrial birds; active, incessantly wagging tail; run or walk brisk; several keep to damp areas and a few perch on trees. **Wagtails** are more colourful; some can be highly gregarious; **Pipits** are duller-plumaged, often streaked.

WARBLERS Large, widespread family of dull-plumaged, small birds of bush, grass-growth, foliage; distinctive call-notes of several species; some have long tail; many, especially Leaf-warblers, difficult to identify in field; predominantly insectivorous.

WEAVERS, MUNIAS & FINCHES Usually gregarious, small birds; some show sexual dimorphism; conical beaks typical of seed-eaters; may feed their young on insects; nests of weavers amongst the finest examples of avian architecture. The Rosefinch often ascends into tall canopy.

WHITE-EYE Tiny, active bird, occ in mixed bird parties; arboreal but also descends into bush.

WOODPECKERS Small to medium-size birds with usually bright plumage; long, dagger-like beak; short wedge-shape tail and modified feet enable clinging and climbing on tree stem, branches; dig nest-cavities in wood; feed mostly on wood-boring insects, larvae; loud screaming calls, characteristic drumming. The **Wryneck** is a cyptic-plumaged bird of scrub and ground.

WOODSHRIKE Small, slightly stocky, dull-plumaged bird; low trees, bush; chiefly insectivorous.

WOODSWALLOWS Medium-size birds of somewhat dumpy appearance; short tail; stout, pointed beak; harsh calls; hawk insects; often in Palmyra-dotted areas.

arboreal: living in trees, especially upper branches

barred: having horizontal bands

cere: bare, usually coloured patch at base of beak, most often in raptors

coverts: smaller feathers

crepuscular: active before dawn or just after dusk

cross-rayed: close-packed, often faint barring as on the tail of some birds

deciduous: forest or trees that are seasonally dry and lose leaves; dominant forest-type in the Mumbai region

drumming: reverberating sound produced by a woodpecker knocking its beak against a tree

eclipse plumage: transitory plumage acquired by certain birds (notably waterfowl) soon after breeding

flight-feathers: large feathers (primaries and secondaries) along rear or trailing-edge of wing; also includes tail-feathers

frugivorous: fruit-eating

fulvous: pale yellow-brown shade

gorget: band across the breast, like a necklace

gular: pertaining to the throat. **Gular stripe** is a darkish stripe down the throat-centre. **Gular pouch** is a loose skin-patch

hackles: slender, longish feathers on/around neck (Grey Junglefowl)

hepatic: rufous phase in certain female cuckoos

juvenile (juv): young bird out of the nest

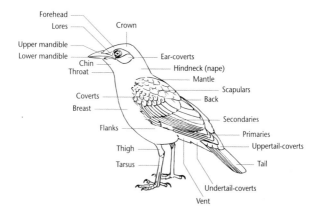

lores: small area between eye and beak

mantle: combined area of upperbody that includes back, scapulars and upperwing-coverts

mesial stripe: stripe along centre or middle (throat)

nuchal: pertaining to neck, usually referring to collar

orbital-patch: bare area around eye-ring

passerines: perching birds (the most dominant group) including song-birds

pectoral tufts: small feathers on the breast-sides (male sunbirds)

primaries: largest, longest feathers along the wing-tips that constitute the flight-feathers, along with **secondaries**

raptor: a bird of prey (eagle, hawk, falcon)

scapulars: wing shoulders

speculum: glossy band across secondaries (waterfowl)

storey: layer or level of forest (lower, middle and upper)

supercilium: eyebrow

tarsus: long, bare part of hind leg

underwings: under-surface of wings as seen in overhead flight

vent: area close to the undertail-coverts

vermiculated: finely marked with thin bars or lines, usually wavy (nightjars, wryneck)

vinaceous: wine-red colour

wing-bar: band or bands across upperwing (can be pale or dark)

wintering sites: usually southern sites to which birds migrate during winter

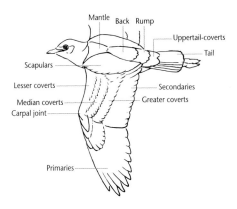

This pocket-guide is divided into three main sections: Wetlands, Forest, Grass & Scrub; a smaller, fourth section includes Urban Areas of the region.

Species found in one **habitat** are often present in other habitats as well. Such overlaps are indicated with a habitat-specific icon as under:

- Wetlands
- Forests
- Grass & Scrub
- Urban Areas

The **size** of each bird has been determined by measuring its length in inches from the tip of its beak to the tip of its tail. A brief yardstick:

4-5"	smaller than House Sparrow
6"	House Sparrow
9-10"	Common Myna
13"	Rock Pigeon
16-17"	House Crow
21-24"	Domestic Duck
23-25"	Black Kite

The **places listed** alongside each entry are the best sites (in order of preference) where the species can be seen.

Females have been depicted in some **illustrations**, especially for species where there is a marked difference in plumage between the sexes. This marked difference is also highlighted with the words 'Sexes differ'. Juveniles have not been depicted.

The words **Common**, **Fairly common**, **Uncommon** and **Scarce** refer to the **status** of the species in the region.

The following abbreviations pertain to the seasonal or year-round **presence** of a species in the region:

BV Breeding Visitor (usually monsoon)

LM Local Migrant; moves locally (eg from Deccan to Konkan, etc)

PM Passage Migrant; makes a brief stopover in the region *en route* to wintering or breeding areas. Most PMs are observed during Sept-Nov and again during Mar-Apr

R Resident; is present year round (actual nest found or

adequate evidence of species breeding in the region)

WV Winter Visitor (mostly mid-Sept to April)

PLUMAGE

Plumage described pertains to adult male birds unless female and juvenile are specifically mentioned.

Female plumage is described for species in which sexes differ.

Juvenile (Juv) plumage is described in cases where young bird sightings are likely.

OH flight refers to the bird as seen from below in overhead flight (ie flying above observer).

In flight refers to the bird as seen in flight, in profile or from above.

Diagnostic refers to a 'give-away' feature that best helps to identify the bird. The most important or diagnostic features/calls/habits of each bird are highlighted in bold.

HABITS

This information provides brief pointers about the bird's behaviour, preference for a particular terrain, etc.

CALL

Bird-calls and songs are not easy to express in words and interpretations can vary. As far as possible, easy-to-understand phonetic syllables and metaphors have been used to express various calls. The first call mentioned refers to year-round, common call-notes of the bird. Other calls noted are specific seasonal or alarm-notes. No reference to a call indicates that no significant call of the species has been recorded in the region. Certain species do not have a true call/voice (eg Storks).

♪ Implies that this species has a diagnostic call or song that can help greatly in identifying the bird.

RELATED

These are species that bear a close resemblance to the main bird listed.

The KNOW YOUR BIRDS section provides information on key characteristics of a bird group or family.

Names used follow *An Annotated Checklist of the Birds of the Oriental Region* by Inskipp, Lindsey & Duckworth (1996).

WETLANDS

Coastal and inland wetlands: sandy, rocky beaches, mudflats, estuaries, creeks, bays, reedy marshes, ponds, lakes, reservoirs.

Elephanta
Sewri Bay
Uran 1 (From start of Palm Beach Rd to Jasai)
Uran 2 (From Jasai to Uran marshes, Funde, Panje)

CREEKS
Bassein Creek, Dharamtar Creek, Mahim Creek
Makunsar Creek, Malad Creek (incl BMC lagoon)
Manori Creek, Murud Creek, Revdanda Creek
Thane Creek (incl Navi Mumbai area, Godrej mangroves)

MARSHES
MB marshes (Mira-Bhayandar)
Naigon-Bassein
RFM (Rain-filled marshes – seasonal)
Talzan (Charkop-Talzan)

LAKES & PONDS
Bhavan's pond
Gorai (incl Manori and Uttan)
Lakes 1 (Vihar, Powai, Tulsi, Tansa, Vaitarna, Barvi)
Lakes 2 (Nilje, Kakuli, Ghoni, Bhoj, Gadeshwar, Panvel, Dhokavne, Devkop, Bandre, Nirmal, Palasdhare, Wavarli, Durshet, others)
Lakes 3 (Lonavala plateau, Malshej top)
Ponds/marshes in **Juhu airfield grounds**
Malvani

COAST
Mumbai (Cuffe Parade to Marve, incl Aksa)
North (Manori-Bassein-Nirmal-Arnala, Datiwere-Kelve-Mahim)
South (Rewas-Mandwa-Kihim-Alibaug-Revdanda-Murud-Agardanda)

LITTLE CORMORANT *Phalacrocorax niger*

20"

Blackish, aquatic bird, larger than House Crow

R

PLUMAGE Blackish with small white patch on chin, throat. **BRDG:** (May-Aug) Jet-black with greenish gloss; **silvery-grey mantle** (scaly, grey and black), **wing-coverts**; some silky-white on fore-crown, sides of head. Juv: Browner; white throat, abdomen. Thicker neck, and shorter head than other cormorants.

All sites
Common

HABITS Usually gregarious; often with Indian Cormorant; **emerges out of water to bask;** may indulge in collective hunting, with much frenetic activity. Breeds in mixed heronries, often in crowded localities.

INDIAN CORMORANT *Phalacrocorax fuscicollis*

25"

Slender, aquatic bird, larger and longer-necked than Little

R

PLUMAGE Dull-yellow gular-patch, often with some white on throat. **BRDG: Metallic bronze-black above; white tuft behind eyes;** sparse white speckling on head, neck. Juv: Brownish above; dingy-white below, mottled. Longer beak than Little and more oval-shaped head.

Most sites
Fairly common

HABITS Gregarious; often with Little.

RELATED GREAT CORMORANT *P carbo* **32"**
Visibly larger, heavier-looking; white cheeks, throat; sighted Panvel, Tulsi Lake (SGNP). Scarce.

LITTLE HERON *Butorides striatus*

17"

Small, thickset, darkish heron of shaded creeks and pools

R/LM

All creeks
Sewri Bay
Elephanta
Bassein Crk
Uncommon

PLUMAGE Grey, black and deep metallic-green above; white cheeks, chin and throat; in flight, **lacks white** in wings and tail; slightly smaller than Pond Heron.

HABITS Normally solitary at edge of creek; **secretive;** keeps to shaded, secluded pools, tidal creeks, often in dense mangrove; periodically emerges in open; occ at inland waterlogged sites during rains.

GREY HERON *Ardea cinerea*

36-39"

Greyish, long-legged bird of open marshes

WV/LM

Uran 1,2
Thane Crk
Sewri Bay
MB marshes
Manori Crk
Elephanta
Lakes 1-3

Fairly common
(Oct-May)

PLUMAGE Pale-grey above; **whitish head, neck; black stripe from behind eyes continues as occipital crest;** yellowish beak; black, speckled band down centre of fore-neck; white below; **in flight, blackish flight-feathers contrast with pale wing-coverts.**

HABITS Often several scattered on marsh or surrounds; sluggish bird, leisurely flight; frequently with other waterbirds but aloof. Call: Occ *kwaarhk* in flight, often when driving an intruding bird from feeding territory.

PURPLE HERON   *Ardea purpurea*

31-35"

Lanky, slender-
necked bird of
reedy marshes

LM/WV

PLUMAGE Slaty-grey above, with black crown
and **long, drooping crest; black stripe along
length of rufous neck;** white chin, throat;
chestnut and grey-black below breast; in flight,
rusty-chestnut underwing-coverts, greyish flight-
feathers and dark tail.

Uran 1,2
MB marshes
Vihar Lk
Lakes 2
Thane Crk
Uncommon
(Oct-Apr)

HABITS Wary and unobtrusive bird of open and
reedy marshes; largely solitary; stands frozen for
long periods, difficult to sight amid reeds.
Call: Occ a high-pitched *grrak* in flight.

INDIAN POND HERON   *Ardeola grayii*

18"

Thickset heron
suddenly
revealing white
in flight

R

PLUMAGE Ashy-brown above; head and neck
darker, with buff-yellow streaking; white chin,
throat; **streaked breast;** in flight, sudden flash
of **white (wings and tail). BRDG:** (rains) **Rich-
maroon back, shoulders;** head and neck buff-
brown; longish, drooping crest.

All sites
also occ
S&C Mumbai
Common

HABITS Usually several in vicinity; often
overlooked when settled, springing to life with
flash of white; definite part of any marshside
scene. Call: A harsh croak in flight; croaking cries
when brdg.

CATTLE EGRET *Bubulcus ibis*

20"

Snow-white
egret often
around cattle
or on garbage
dumps

R

All sites
Common

PLUMAGE Snowy-white, with **yellow beak**.
BRDG: **(Apr-Aug) Buff golden-orange plumes** on
head, neck and back. Overall less lanky than all
other white herons.

HABITS Usually gregarious, often large
gatherings on landfills; attends to grazing cattle,
grass-cutters, agricultural activity; often away
from water; may be seen in forest (SGNP,
Karnala) picking out cicadas during peak
summer; also in urban areas. Call: Various
croaking notes at heronry.

LITTLE EGRET *Egretta garzetta*

25"

Slender, snow-
white water bird
with yellow toes

R/LM

Most sites
Fairly common

PLUMAGE White; **diagnostic black beak, legs;
yellow toes**. **BRDG:** (rains) Nuchal crest of
2 long plumes on head, besides ornamental,
filamentous feathers on back and breast. Can be
confused with white phase of Western Reef Egret
but black beak and longish legs help distinguish.

HABITS Solitary or several, often with other
waders; hunting style typical of herons; occ
indulges in jumping and 'dancing' in water,
possibly to disturb prey. Call: An occ croaking
call in flight.

GREAT EGRET *Casmerodius albus*   36"

PLUMAGE Snow-white overall; **bare, yellow-green facial skin**; yellowish beak, black legs and toes. **BRDG**: (rains) Beak mostly black, with bluish lores; may show some yellow on lower mandible; **black line of gape stretching behind eye; decorative plumes only on back.**

HABITS Few birds over a stretch of marsh; occ solitary; wades in water, often several inches deep; somewhat territorial even when feeding. Call: Loud croaking cry in flight, often when driving intruder from feeding territory.

Lanky, snow-white marsh-bird, with kink in neck
R/LM

Uran 1,2
All creeks
Vihar Lk
Powai Lk
Coast-N,S
Uncommon
(very few breed)

INTERMEDIATE EGRET *Egretta intermedia*   26"

PLUMAGE Snow-white. **BRDG**: (rains) **Plumes on back and upper-breast; dark gape-line ends below eyes.** Size not reliable pointer of identification; neck distinctly shorter than Great.

HABITS Somewhat more gregarious than Great; often with other herons.

(inset) Lanky, snow-white, often social marsh bird
R/LM

Most sites
Fairly common
(few breed)

WESTERN REEF EGRET *Egretta gularis*

23"

Lanky, white or slaty-grey heron of coastal areas

WV

Coast-N,S
Sewri Bay
Thane Crk
Manori Crk
Dharamtar Crk
occ S Mumbai
coast
Uncommon
(mostly Nov-Apr)

PLUMAGE 2 distinct colour phases.
DARK: Deep slaty-grey overall; white throat.
LIGHT: Whitish overall; **quite similar to Little Egret**, also with **yellowish toes (but duller)**; legs never pure black; beak may have some yellow.
BRDG: Ornamental plumes as in Little Egret (sighted once N Mumbai coast).

HABITS Invariably on rocky or sandy coast; solitary or pairs; occ 3-4 birds over length of coast; **sluggish and wary**; sometimes wades deep; may feed well past dusk. **Call:** Occ hoarse croak in flight.

BLACK-CROWNED NIGHT HERON *Nycticorax nycticorax*

23-25"

Stocky, grey, black and white heron, often hunched

R

Most sites
RFM
Common
(breeds Apr-Aug)

PLUMAGE Blackish crown, nape and drooping crest with few long white plumes; **dark mantle has variable metallic-green gloss**; white cheeks, short stripe over eye; pale ashy-white below; **blood-red eyes**, yellow-green feet; in flight, **grey wings, tail. Juv:** Brown, much-streaked.

HABITS Nocturnal and crepuscular; **best observed at dusk** when small parties fly to favoured feeding sites (marshes, also forest streams as in SGNP); spends day in leafy trees. **Call:** Distinctive, raucous *kwock* in flight.

CINNAMON BITTERN *Ixobrychus cinnamomeus*

15"

Secretive, tawny-chestnut heron of reed beds. Sexes differ

R/LM

PLUMAGE Cinnamon (tawny-rufous) above; rufous-chestnut flight-feathers; paler below; at close range, **white chin, throat,** dark stripe down centre of fore-neck. Female: **Deep rufous-brown above, darker on crown;** rufous-buff below, **streaked.** Juv: Deep-brown above, mottled; streaked below.

Uran 1,2
MB marshes
Talzan
Ghoni Lk
Powai Lk
Vihar Lk
RFM
Fairly common

HABITS Secretive and crepuscular; several around but mostly seen when flying low over marshes, flooded paddy-fields; more visible during rains (brdg). Call: Courting male has loud *kock-kok* cry; also a harsh *kwark*.

YELLOW BITTERN *Ixobrychus sinensis*

15"

Dull-coloured, secretive bird of reed beds

R/LM

PLUMAGE Pale yellow-brown with **blackish crown** and fuzzy crest; dull-vinaceous sides of face, neck; dull-white chin, throat, fore-neck; buff below; in flight, **black flight-feathers, tail.** Juv: Buff above, **streaked darker;** streaked rufous-buff below.

MB marshes
Naigon-Bassein
Uran 1,2
Talzan
Ghoni Lk
RFM
Uncommon

HABITS Prefers reed beds, wet cultivation; solitary or pairs; secretive and crepuscular; often overlooked; like other bitterns, active during day in overcast weather. Call: Occ a soft *kaak* in low flight.

PAINTED STORK *Mycteria leucocephala*

38–40"

Large, whitish, aquatic bird with black and pink in wings

LM/WV

Uran 1,2
Thane Crk
MB marshes
Lakes 1,3
Uncommon

PLUMAGE Largely white; much black on wings; **diagnostic rose-pink wash on greater-coverts; orange-yellow beak, bare face; pink-red legs; OH flight, extensive black on underwings;** diffused breast-band contrasts with white neck and abdomen. Juv: Pale, dingy-brown overall.

HABITS Small flocks (max 40 birds sighted Uran); often with other waterbirds, moving in deeper waters; sometimes soars (sighted Uran, MB marshes).

ASIAN OPENBILL *Anastomus oscitans*

26–28"

Small, dull-white stork with peculiar beak

LM/WV

Uran 1,2
MB marshes
Lakes 1,3
Thane Crk
Uncommon

PLUMAGE Dull, smoky-white overall; purple-green sheen on **black of wings, tail; in OH flight,** black flight-feathers, dull-white underwing-coverts, underbody; **diagnostic beak, long and thick with wide gap along centre of** mandibles; **pinkish legs.** Juv: Dark smoky-brown.

HABITS Small gatherings, often with other waterbirds; peculiar gap in beak helps feed on molluscs; soars with other large birds.

WHITE STORK *Ciconia ciconia*

40-46"

Tall, white and black bird with red beak and legs

WV

PLUMAGE White with **extensive black on wings; bright-red legs, large, pointed beak.**

HABITS Solitary or 3-8 at edge of marshes, cultivation, occ tidal areas; moves cautiously, rarely with other waterbirds.

RELATED WOOLLY-NECKED STORK *Ciconia episcopus* White neck, contrasts with glossy-black plumage; reddish legs; dark beak; occ in cultivation, rain-filled depressions, reservoirs; sporadically Uran, outskirts of Mumbai; once on small pond in Lion Safari, SGNP. Uncommon.

Thane Crk
Uran 1,2
Scarce

Much declined since early-1980s. Recently reported Thane Crk, Uran 2

EURASIAN SPOONBILL *Platalea leucorodia*

32-34"

White bird with flattened, spoon-shaped beak

LM/WV

PLUMAGE Snow-white overall, with small yellow-brown patch at base of fore-neck; blackish **beak, long, flat and spatula-shaped,** yellow towards broader, spoon-like tip; black legs.
BRDG: (occ post-rains) Fluffy, nuchal crest.

HABITS Chiefly inland marshes; once Thane Creek; small gatherings (over 100 sighted at Uran); amid wader congregations on favoured marshes (Uran area); **wades actively in shallow water, sweeping beak to pick food.**

Uran 2
Thane Crk
Lakes 3
Uncommon

BLACK-HEADED IBIS *Threskiornis melanocephalus*

30"

Long-legged white bird with black head and decurved beak

LM/WV

Uran 1,2
Thane Crk
Lakes 1&3
Uncommon

PLUMAGE White overall, with **naked black head, legs** and **diagnostic, long, down-curved beak;** some slaty-grey in outer flight-feathers; **in OH flight, maroon-red patches on underwings, flanks. BRDG:** (occ seen Sep-Nov) Plume-like feathers around base of neck, upper-breast; tertiaries longer, appearing decorative.

HABITS Open marshes; often several around with other waterbirds; feeds in soft, slimy mud in shallow water; moves rapidly; settles on trees.

GLOSSY IBIS *Plegadis falcinellus*

22-25"

Slender, maroon-brown marsh bird with long, curved beak

WV

Uran 1,2
Thane Crk
Lakes 1&3
Scarce

PLUMAGE Feathered head. Dull maroon-brown above, with variable purplish-green gloss; at close range, faint, whitish streaking about neck, head. **BRDG:** Deep chestnut-maroon with purple-green gloss. Juv: Dark-brown.

HABITS Keeps to well-watered marshes; small gatherings; occ large flocks (up to 200 sighted Uran); sometimes with other waterbirds.

RELATED BLACK IBIS *Pseudibis papillosa* Slightly larger; white shoulder-patch; bare, bright-red on crown. Highly uncommon.

GREATER FLAMINGO *Phoenicopterus ruber*

PLUMAGE Rosy-white overall; **black and scarlet in wings** (black primaries, outer secondaries); sharply **down-curved**, **large**, **pink beak, tipped black**. In flight, outstretched pink legs and neck. Juv: Grey-brown.

HABITS Highly gregarious, **often thousands together**; when not feeding, often rests on one leg, neck coiled and head tucked in feathers. Enormous gatherings of Greater and Lesser Flamingo seen at Sewri Bay and Thane Creek since early-1990s. Call: Mumbling cries when feeding; also a loud, far-reaching honk.

RELATED **LESSER FLAMINGO** *P minor* **40"** Smaller, with proportionately shorter neck; **deeper rose-pink plumage; red legs, deep crimson-black beak**, smaller and more conspicuously curled; deep-crimson eyes and small facial-patch; in recent years, commoner than Greater at Sewri. Common.

50-54"
Long-legged,
long-necked,
rose-white bird
with striking beak
WV

Sewri Bay
Thane Crk
Coast-N
occ Uran 2,
Aksa, Manori Crk
Common
(Oct-May)

LITTLE GREBE *Tachybaptus ruficollis*

10"

Squat, tailless waterbird. Smallest duck-like bird in the region

R/LM (rains)

Lakes 1-3
MB marshes
occ creeks
Fairly Common

PLUMAGE Pale-brown above, with paler cheeks; **whitish chin, throat, small patch on flight-feathers. BRDG:** (Jun-Sep) Deeper-brown above; **rufous-chestnut cheeks, fore-neck, throat.** Juv: (seen Jul-Nov) White streaks on sides of head.

HABITS Pairs or several scattered on water; rapid flight, usually low; great skulker with preference for vegetation-fringed freshwater sites. Call: Distinctive; a shrill pleasing trill; more vocal when brdg; occ a sharp *click* or *wheet*.

LESSER WHISTLING-DUCK *Dendrocygna javanica*

17"

Rufous-brown duck with diagnostic whistling call
R/LM

Uran 1,2
All creeks
Lakes 1-3
MB marshes
Fairly common

PLUMAGE Rufous-brown, feathers on back margined with fulvous; dark-brown crown and paler, buff-grey head, neck; **in flight, diagnostic chestnut uppertail-coverts, forewing-patch;** dark-brown flight-feathers. Juv: Duller overall.

HABITS Gregarious; during summer/winter, rests by day in creek-channels, lakes or open sea; flies along fixed routes to feeding areas (marshes, lakes) around dusk; feeds during night; breeds inland during rains. Call: Diagnostic, 2-noted whistling call, often indicative of bird's presence in and/or flying over an area.

SPOT-BILLED DUCK *Anas poecilorhyncha*

24"

Scaly-patterned, grey-brown duck with yellow-tipped beak

R/LM

PLUMAGE Profusely scaly-patterned, brownish; dark crown, stripe through eyes; **diagnostic yellow-tipped black beak**; in flight, **metallic-green speculum**, bordered by black and white bands.

MB marshes
Lakes 1-3
Uran 2
occ Coast-S
also occ Aarey
Uncommon

HABITS Inland marshes, lakes, preferably shallow, vegetation-covered; usually few around; pairs seen May-Sep in flooded paddy-fields; surface-feeder; strong flier. **Call:** Occ loud quack when disturbed; male also has harsh, wheezy note.

COMB DUCK *Sarkidiornis melanotos*

30"

Large black and white duck with peculiar top of beak. Sexes differ

R/LM

PLUMAGE Black back, glossed with purple-green; **white head, neck, freckled with black**; pale-white below, with black half-collar on breast-sides; **diagnostic fleshy knob (comb)** at forehead, near base of beak. **Female:** Smaller, paler; **lacks fleshy comb**. **Juv:** Variable brownish-rufous in plumage (sighted Vaitarna, Nirmal pond).

Lakes 1-3
Uran 2
Uncommon

HABITS Inland marshes, lakes; pairs or small parties; occ enters paddy-fields, sometimes around forest; also perches on trees; nests in tree-hollows. **Call:** Occ harsh croak.

COTTON PYGMY-GOOSE *Nettapus coromandelianus*

13"

Small duck with contrasting black and white plumage. Sexes differ

R/LM

Uran 2
Lakes 1-3
MB marshes
Juhu airfield
Uncommon

PLUMAGE Glossy-black above; blackish cap; white face, neck, underbody; blackish neck-collar; in flight, **pied plumage, with extensive white (broad band) in wings. Female:** Paler overall; lacks white wing-band, black collar. Non brdg Male: Duller overall.

HABITS Vegetation-covered inland marshes, lakes; pairs or small parties, often by themselves, sometimes quite confiding; largely surface-feeder; flies fast, usually low but may rise to top of average-size trees. Call: Occ an abrupt, shrill *whee-whaeuu* in flight (heard MB marshes).

NORTHERN PINTAIL *Anas acuta*

22"

Long-necked, surface-feeding duck with long, pointed tail. Sexes differ

WV

Uran 2
Lakes 1-3
MB marshes
occ Thane,
Manori,
Malad Crks
Fairly common
(common
some years)

PLUMAGE Pale-grey above, with choco-brown head; white stripe down neck-sides to white breast; **long tail with pin-like central feathers, up to 4-5" long;** in flight, green speculum, bordered white; in OH flight, pointed tail, dark head, slender neck and white underbody. **Female:** Mottled buff-brown; pointed tail lacks long central feathers.

HABITS Gregarious; often amid other waterfowl.

GARGANEY *Anas querquedula*

16"

Small duck with
white stripe
on head.
Sexes differ

WV

**PLUMAGE Diagnostic broad white stripe
on brownish head**, pale-brown, speckled
breast; in flight, **blue-grey coverts**, **green
speculum** bordered with white bands; **OH flight**,
dark breast, pale (occ whitish) underbody.
Female: Brown above, scalloped paler; striped
head-pattern; duller-green speculum.

Uran 2
Lakes 1-3
MB marshes
occ creeks
Common

HABITS Inland marshes, lakes; occ creeks; small
parties with other waterfowl; typical surface-
feeder; **swift, sprightly flight**. Call: Occ a short,
quick quack.

GADWALL *Anas strepera*

19"

Small, greyish
duck with
white belly and
white in wings.
Sexes differ

WV

PLUMAGE Grey and dull-brown overall, with
diagnostic black tail-end (stern); in flight,
dull-chestnut wing-coverts and white on rear
of wings, bordered with black; **OH flight**, white
belly, black undertail, white in wings.
Female: Mottled-brown; white wing-patch helps
separate from female Pintail, Mallard; **diagnostic
orangish sides of beak**.

Lakes 1-3
MB marshes
Uran 2
Fairly common

HABITS Small flocks, sometimes amid other
waterfowl; typical dabbling duck.

NORTHERN SHOVELER *Anas clypeata*

20"

Duck with massive, spatulate beak. Sexes differ

WV

Uran 2
Lakes 1-3
Uncommon

PLUMAGE Glossy-green head; white breast, **chestnut belly;** in flight, conspicuous **blue shoulder-patches,** white band and metallic-green speculum; **in OH flight, dark head, white neck, dark-chestnut belly and flanks.** Female: Profusely mottled brown and buff; pale-blue shoulder-patch; dull-green speculum.

HABITS Chiefly inland marshes; small loose bands with other dabbling ducks; **huge beak held close to water or partly immersed;** also feeds on wet ground. Call: Occ fairly loud quack, 2-noted call in flight.

RUDDY SHELDUCK *Tadorna ferruginea*

25-27"

Large, orangish duck. Sexes differ slightly

WV

Uran 2
Thane Crk
Powai (once)
Uncommon

PLUMAGE Bright orange-rufous; pale-buff head, neck; blackish neck-collar; in flight metallic-green speculum and large, **white patch on wing-coverts;** in OH flight, **orange-chestnut underbody,** dark flight-feathers and white underwings. Female: Paler head; lacks black neck-collar.

HABITS Open, inland marshes, lakes; usually small parties (max 35 sighted Uran); alert and wary; partial to shallow waters. Call: 2-noted, nasal honking *awh-onk* or *awng-awng*.

COMMON TEAL *Anas crecca*

15"

Small, pale-grey duck with dark-chestnut and green head. Sexes differ

WV

PLUMAGE Pale-grey above; **diagnostic chestnut head with broad metallic-green stripe from eye to nape**; white stripe along scapulars; in flight, black and metallic-green speculum bordered with buff-white; **in OH flight, dark head, pale underbody.** Female: Buff and brown, speckled; **green and black speculum** helps differentiate from Garganey.

Uran 2
Lakes 1-3
MB marshes
Fairly common

HABITS Inland marshes; occ brackish water (Uran); usually small gatherings with other waterfowl. **Call:** Various nasal cries when feeding; a distinctive, short *kkrrit-krrit* of male.

COMMON POCHARD *Aythya ferina*

18"

High-crowned, dark-headed duck of open water. Sexes differ

WV

PLUMAGE Deep-chestnut head, neck; black breast; in flight, **dark head, fore-body, pale-greyish wings, dark tail;** in OH flight, dark head, breast, pale belly and dark tail. Female: Pale ashy-brown above, darker head.

Uran 2
Lakes 1,3
Uncommon

HABITS Open lakes, reservoirs, even deep waters; shy and watchful; patters on surface before taking off on strong flight.

FERRUGINOUS POCHARD *Aythya nyroca*

16"

Dark-brown
duck with white
in wings.
Sexes differ

WV

Uran 2
occ Gorai,
Alibaug, Kelve
Uncommon

PLUMAGE Deep-brown above with **chestnut-brown head**, neck and breast; **conspicuous white eyes**; white undertail-coverts may be visible at rest; white flight-feathers; **in OH flight, dark head, breast contrast with white underwings, belly.** Female: Duller; brown eyes.

HABITS Spends day resting in deeper waters, occ on open sea, beyond the surf; also open lakes, reservoirs; shy and wary; often overlooked.

BRAHMINY KITE *Haliastur indus*

19"

Bright-chestnut
and white raptor

R/LM

● ● ●

Most sites
Fairly common
(few breed)

PLUMAGE Bright **rust-chestnut**, with **white head**, neck and breast; OH flight, diagnostic; brighter-chestnut wing-lining (coverts) and paler-rufous flight-feathers contrast with **blackish tips to primaries**. Juv: Brownish, with variable, buff-rufous on underwings; roundish tail.

HABITS Inland and coastal waters; solitary, pairs or several scattered over an area, circling or perched on trees, poles; often scavenges. Call: Occ a loud gasping scream, usually in flight.

EURASIAN MARSH HARRIER *Circus aeruginosus*

20-23"

Brownish, low-flying, marsh-side raptor. Sexes differ

WV

PLUMAGE Dark-brown above, with **streaked, dull rufous-buff head, neck, upper-breast**; rufous below; **grey tail; much grey in dark-tipped wings**, visible at rest and in flight. Female: Dark choco-brown; **pale-buff crown**, throat; **buff on wing-shoulders** (at rest and in flight). Juv: Head dark-brown or like female.

HABITS Reedy marshes, lakes, lagoons, creeks; often solitary, sometimes pairs; glides low; leisurely flight; pounces to seize prey. Call: Shrill *kweeeuh*, often when settled on treetop or in marsh; other shrill notes.

Uran 1,2
Lakes 1-3
MB marshes
All creeks
Fairly common

WHITE-BELLIED SEA EAGLE *Haliaeetus leucogaster*

28"

Large, ashy-brown and white coastal raptor

R/LM

PLUMAGE Ashy-brown above, with **white head, neck; white below; in OH flight**, white body, broad, wings with blackish flight-feathers, **broad, white terminal band on wedge-shaped tail**. Juv: Brown and dull-tawny; paler head.

HABITS Solitary or pairs, rarely several together (11 birds once scattered along 1 km stretch over Manori-Gorai); **stoops from perch, legs outstretched to snatch prey** from water; has favourite feeding perches. Call: Loud nasal screams; very vocal when brdg (Oct–Feb). Makes huge nests in Casuarina trees.

Coast-N,S
Elephanta
Lakes 1
All creeks
Nirmal (once)
Uncommon

OSPREY *Pandion haliaetus*

22"

Dark-brown and white raptor found around water

WV

Uran 2
Lakes 1, 3
All creeks
Elephanta
Coast-N
Uncommon

PLUMAGE Deep-brownish above; **white about head**; dark eye-stripe; **white below**, with indistinct, dark breast-band; in **OH flight, white underbody**, faint breast-band, **pale, longish, angled wings**, with white underwing-coverts, dark tips and carpal-patches; barred, squarish tail.

HABITS Inland and coastal waters; usually solitary, rarely pairs; circles 10-15 m over water; intermittently hovers, dives headlong with wings closed, occ going under; catches fish in talons; may have favourite feeding perches. Call: Occ a sharp whistling cry.

SLATY-BREASTED RAIL *Gallirallus striatus*

10-11"

Secretive slaty-blue and rufous-chestnut bird

R

Uran 1,2
Lakes 1-3
MB marshes
Thane Crk
Juhu airfield
RFM

Fairly common

PLUMAGE Dark-brown above, lightly speckled white; **rufous-chestnut crown, neck-sides; slaty-blue breast, sides of face**; barred abdomen, flanks; olive-grey legs and feet. Female: Duller above.

HABITS Vegetation-covered marshes, lake-edges, creeks; largely solitary; secretive, skulking; often overlooked; occ emerges at edge of marsh; often walks upright, jerking tail, scampering into cover on slightest disturbance. Call: Occ soft scream.

SLATY-LEGGED CRAKE *Rallina eurizonoides*

10"

Dark-brown marsh bird with long, greyish legs

R/LM

PLUMAGE Olivish-brown above; **rufous-chestnut head, neck and breast**; white chin, throat; **banded blackish-brown and white below breast; slaty legs.** Juv: Dark olive-brown above, incl head.

Lakes 3
occ Coast-S
Uncommon

HABITS Marshy areas around forest, often in hilly areas; solitary or pairs; **elusive and secretive**; often overlooked; may settle on trees when flushed. Call: Highly vocal (brdg, rains); longish drumming and various call-notes; loud, harsh, 2-noted *khae-khek*; occ through night.

RUDDY-BREASTED CRAKE *Porzana fusca*

8-9"

Small, elusive, dark-brown, red-legged marsh bird

R

PLUMAGE Unmarked, deep olive-brown above; **dark (vinous)-chestnut forehead, sides of face, neck and breast**; whitish chin, throat; chestnut-brown abdomen, flanks; white-barred lower abdomen, undertail-coverts; **reddish legs, feet.**

Uran 1,2
MB marshes
Talzan
Naigon-Bassein
Uncommon

HABITS Vegetation-covered marshes, lake-edges; usually solitary; shy and wary; extremely difficult to observe. Call: An occ *krraek*; possibly soft chuckles; more vocal during rains (brdg).

BAILLON'S CRAKE *Porzana pusilla*

7-8"

Tiny, brown and grey, secretive marsh bird

WV

Uran 1,2
Lakes 1,2
MB marshes
Bhavan's pond
Juhu airfield
Uncommon

PLUMAGE Olivish-brown above, with faint-rufous wash, variably-speckled; **pale slaty-grey below and face-sides; barred brown and white on flanks, undertail; greenish beak, legs and feet.**

HABITS Reedy, vegetation-fringed marshes; also paddy-fields; often solitary; easily overlooked.

RELATED LITTLE CRAKE *P parva* Less rufous above; much less barring on flanks. Female: Paler face; pinkish-buff below; sighted MB marshes, Powai, Malvani, Kihim. Uncommon.

WHITE-BREASTED WATERHEN *Amaurornis phoenicurus*

12"

Blackish rail with conspicuous white front

R

Most sites
occ creeks,
S&C Mumbai
Fairly common

PLUMAGE Deep slaty-grey above (appears blackish); **white forehead, sides of face; white below (chin to abdomen);** rufous-chestnut vent, undertail; yellow-green beak, some red on upper-mandible; large **olive-yellow legs.**

HABITS Vegetation-covered marsh-edges, lakes, rivers; occ creeks; solitary, pairs or scattered parties; **easily observed; emerges in open;** often in vicinity of habitation. Call: Extremely noisy when brdg (rains); harsh, loud chuckling sounds erupting into monotonous *khrr-khwaak-khwakk* or *khuwakk*; may call at night in overcast weather.

WATERCOCK   *Gallicrex cinerea*

15-17"

Skulking, brown or grey-black marsh bird

R/LM

Uran 2
Lakes 1-3
MB marshes
Uncommon

PLUMAGE Brdg Male: **Deep grey-black above,** mottled buff-brown on back, wings; **diagnostic reddish, horn-like shield above forehead; red beak, legs.** Female and non-brdg Male: **Dark buff-brown,** scalloped buff and tawny.

HABITS Vegetation-covered marshes, flooded paddy-fields; pairs or solitary; secretive and wary; often crepuscular. Call: Noisy (rains); loud, booming *kawk* or *kowk* cry, also a loud, resonant *dhoomb-dhoomb*, several times at a stretch.

PURPLE SWAMPHEN   *Porphyrio porphyrio*

18"

Large, purplish-blue marsh bird

R

Uran 1,2
MB marshes
Lakes 1-3
Malvani
Gorai
Fairly common

PLUMAGE **Purplish-blue overall,** with faint lilac wash on back, flanks, belly; stumpy tail, white underneath (visible when flicked); **diagnostic red beak, bare forehead-shield, long legs and large toes.** Female: Forehead-shield slightly smaller. Juv: Duller overall.

HABITS Reed-covered marshes, lake-edges; often several around; conspicuous; often emerges into open or clambers atop dense mass of reeds; flicks short tail often. Call: Very vocal, especially when brdg; various chuckles and screams.

COMMON MOORHEN *Gallinula chloropus*

13"

Dark, slaty-grey bird with white in wings

R/LM

Uran 1,2
Lakes 1-3
MB marshes
Juhu airfield
Fairly common

PLUMAGE Dark slaty-grey above, **with brown wash on back**; white band along flanks (appears like border to closed wings); **slaty-grey below; white undertail-coverts**; greenish-yellow beak and **bright-red forehead-shield**. Juv: Dingy-brown, with dull-green beak.

HABITS Inland marshes, solitary or pairs; small gathering during winter; **swims duck-like or moves rail-like at marsh-edge; wary; weak, low flight when flushed**; strong flier during migration, like several rails. Call: Occ a brusque, harsh *prruck*.

COMMON COOT *Fulica atra*

16"

Blackish waterbird with white beak

WV

Uran 1,2
Lakes 1-3
MB marshes
Fairly common

PLUMAGE Deep slaty-black overall; **diagnostic white beak, forehead shield**; dull-green legs. Juv: Dusky-grey above; pale-brown below; whitish throat.

HABITS Open marshes, lakes; gregarious during winter; pairs or small parties other times; **patters over water surface before flying.** Call: Abrupt chuckling cries; a loud *trraek* occ at night.

GREATER PAINTED-SNIPE *Rostratula benghalensis*

10"

Heavily-patterned, long-billed, secretive marsh bird

R

PLUMAGE Glossy olive-green above, profusely mottled buff and black; **white spectacles, stripe behind eye**; olive-brown breast; white below. Brdg Female: **Bronze-green above, marked buff; white eye-stripe; diagnostic chestnut-maroon face-sides, throat, upper-breast,** bordered by black band; white below.

HABITS Pairs usually close by; chiefly crepuscular, nocturnal; difficult to observe and flush.
Call: More vocal during rains (brdg); a longish *ooohk*, somewhat resonant in tone; may call continuously several times.

Uran 1,2
MB marshes
Lakes 1-3
Juhu airfield
Malvani
Gorai
Naigon-Bassein
Fairly common

PHEASANT-TAILED JACANA *Hydrophasianus chirurgus*

12"

Long-tailed waterbird with very long toes

R

PLUMAGE Black, yellowish and white face, head; black breast-band joined to black stripe along neck-sides; **white underbody. BRDG:** Glossy olive-brown back; white face, fore-neck, upper-breast; **shiny, golden-yellow nape; extensive white in wings;** deep choco-brown below; **sickle-shaped, dark, long, pointed tail.**

HABITS Vegetation-covered marshes, ponds; often several together; daintily moves on surface vegetation; gently-flapping flight, low over water.
Call: Loud, mewing *teoun* or *ptoun*; noisy when brdg (May-Sep).

Uran 2
MB marshes
Lakes 1-3
Malvani
Gorai
Naigon-Bassein
also occ
suburban Mumbai
Fairly common

BRONZE-WINGED JACANA *Metopidius indicus*

11"

Darkish, unobtrusive marsh bird with huge toes

R

♪

Uran 2
Lakes 1-3
MB marshes
RFM
Uncommon

PLUMAGE Bronze-green above; **glossy-black head**, neck, much of underbody; **white supercilium**; short, chestnut tail. Juv: Dull olive-brown above, more rufous on crown, nape.

HABITS Vegetation-covered marshes, ponds; solitary or pairs; often with various rails; less showy overall than Pheasant-tailed. Call: A discordant, high-pitched *tseek-tseeek* in low flight or when settled; more vocal when brdg (rains).

EURASIAN OYSTERCATCHER *Haematopus ostralegus*

17"

Black and white shore bird with reddish legs and beak

WV

Coast-N,S
occ Madh-Aksa
(Mumbai coast)
Uncommon

PLUMAGE Jet-black above; white below breast; in flight, black head, back, wings with **broad white wing-bar**; white rump and **tail with black terminal band; diagnostic orange-red beak and pinkish-red legs.**

HABITS Conspicuous wader on sandy and rocky coast; small flocks; wary, rarely allowing close approach. Call: Calls intermittently; a fairly loud *pick* or *peick*; also a whistling *kleep* or *pleep*, somewhat melancholy in tone.

RUDDY TURNSTONE *Arenaria interpres*

9"
Stocky wader with orangish-red legs
WV

PLUMAGE Dusky-brown above; dark fore-neck, breast-sides; white below; in flight, **diagnostic black and white banded wings, tail**. Stocky appearance and short, black beak. **BRDG:** (occ Apr) Bright rufous-chestnut above; black and white head.

Coast-N,S
Elephanta
occ Madh-Aksa
(Mumbai coast)

Uncommon

HABITS Rocky and sandy coast, mudflats; small parties, by themselves or with other waders; actively turns over shells, small stones; rests amid rocky stretches. **Call:** A rapidly-uttered *trr-tuk-tuk* when flushed.

Much declined on Mumbai coast

LITTLE RINGED PLOVER *Charadrius dubius*

6"
Small, brownish wader with noticeable head pattern
LM/WV

PLUMAGE **Diagnostic black and white head-pattern** (paler overall during winter); sandy-brown above; **black and white hind-collar**; white below, with **black gorget; yellow eye-ring; dull-yellow legs**.

Most sites
Fairly common

Brdg plumage seen around lakes at Malshej, Lonavala

HABITS Marsh-edges, coastal tracts; usually several close by, by themselves or amid other waders; active and busy. **Call:** A sharp *teeyu* or *tee-u*, uttered in flight; short, trilling song (Mar-Jun).

KENTISH PLOVER *Charadrius alexandrinus*

6"

Small, pale-sandy wader with black on breast-sides

LM/WV

Uran 1,2
Coast-N,S
Thane Crk
Manori Crk
Lakes 3
Fairly common

Brdg plumage seen at Pimpalgaon reservoir, Malshej

PLUMAGE Sandy-brown above (paler than Little Ringed); **white forehead, short supercilium, hind-collar; incomplete gorget;** white below; **in flight, narrow, white wing-bar;** blackish beak and legs. **Brdg Male:** (Mar-Aug) **Pale-rufous cap** with small black patch; black eye-stripe, incomplete gorget.

HABITS Margins of wetlands, reservoirs; usually several scattered; active and restless. **Call:** Various soft calls; a piping *too-eet*, a faint but rapid *chrr* and a melodious *wh-tchi*, occ rolled into one another.

GREY PLOVER *Pluvialis squatarola*

11"

Heavy-looking, pale grey-brown coastal wader

WV

Coast-N,S
Uran 1,2
Thane Crk
Manori Crk
Sewri Bay
Fairly common

PLUMAGE Pale brownish-grey above, scalloped paler, whitish below, marked grey-brown on breast, flanks; **in flight, pale-whitish wing-bar, whiter rump, uppertail-coverts; black axillaries.** Short, stout beak. **BRDG:** (*c.* mid/end-Apr) **Silvery grey-black above, profusely white-spangled; black below.**

HABITS Sandy coast, estuaries, brackish marshes; small gatherings, occ with other waders; settles hunched, wary. **Call:** A low, whistling *tle-ooee*, rapidly uttered, mostly in flight.

PACIFIC GOLDEN PLOVER *Pluvialis fulva*

10"

Short-billed
wader, speckled
with pale golden-
yellow above

WV

PLUMAGE Brown above, speckled, **pale-golden and buff-white above**; dull-white below, mottled buff and brown; **in flight, lacks white wing-bar and rump-patch. BRDG:** (*c.* mid/end-Apr) Diagnostic, **more vividly mottled golden-yellow**; white band divides upperbody from jet-black underbody.

HABITS Inland marshes, marsh-edges, creeks; occ paddy-fields; usually small parties; wary and sluggish. **Call:** Fairly high-pitched, brisk *klee-ee* or *tlu-ee*, chiefly in flight.

Uran 1,2
Coast-N,S
Thane Crk
Manori Crk
Uncommon

LESSER SAND PLOVER *Charadrius mongolus*

7"

Small, gregarious,
sandy-brown,
coastal wader

WV

PLUMAGE Sandy-brown above; narrow, white supercilium, browner ear-coverts; in flight, **narrow white wing-bar. BRDG: Rusty-chestnut and black head pattern, breast**; white throat, belly.

HABITS Chiefly sandy and rocky coast; tidal mudflats at low-tide; gregarious, often most numerous on beach; active and busy. **Call:** A subdued but musical *chweip* in low flight.

RELATED GREATER SAND PLOVER *C leschenaultii* Slightly larger; browner above, paler legs. **BRDG:** Rufous and black on head. Fairly common.

Coast-N,S
occ creeks,
Uran 1,2
Common

SANDERLING *Calidris alba*

8"

Active, pale-plumaged, coastal wader

WV

Sewri Bay
Thane Crk
Coast-N,S
Elephanta
Uncommon

PLUMAGE Pale grey-white; **distinctive small, black shoulder-patch**; white below; in flight, pale upperbody, **white band on darker wings**; whitish sides to rump, tail. Short black beak and legs. **BRDG:** (occ late-Apr) Rufous-chestnut above, breast; speckled blackish.

HABITS Sandy coast; occ mudflats; usually gregarious; extremely active, quick-moving, appearing to 'chase' waves. **Call:** Shrill, short *kwit-kwit* when flushed.

EURASIAN CURLEW *Numenius arquata*

22-24"

Large wader with very long, decurved beak

WV

Uran 2
Thane Crk
Sewri Bay
Manori Crk
Coast-N,S
Elephanta
Uncommon

Much declined

PLUMAGE Grey-brown above, profusely streaked and scalloped; dull-whitish below, streaked on throat, breast; **in flight, white on lower back, rump; diagnostic, down-curved, very long beak.**

HABITS Solitary or few around; wild and wary. **Call:** Diagnostic; loud, ringing, rather doleful *coour-le* or *coour-li*; rises in pitch to suddenly drop towards end; occ heard here.

RELATED WHIMBREL *N phaeopus* Smaller; shorter beak; **boldly-striped crown**; in flight, whitish rump. Uncommon. *See inset*

BLACK-TAILED GODWIT *Limosa limosa*

16-19"

Tall, upright, long-billed wader

WV

PLUMAGE Ashy-brown above, paler head; in flight, **broad, white wing-bar, uppertail-coverts; diagnostic black tail-tip**; legs project extensively beyond tail; **dull orange-red, very long, straight beak. BRDG:** (early/mid-Apr) **Rufous-chestnut head, neck, breast; paler below, barred dark on flanks.**

HABITS Freshwater marshes, tidal creeks; active and gregarious, often with other waders; wades up to belly. **Call:** Fairly loud *wheeka-wheeka* in flight; also a nasal *tue-it*.

Uran 1,2
Thane Crk
Sewri Bay
Coast-N,S
Elephanta
Fairly common

BAR-TAILED GODWIT *Limosa lapponica*

16"

Tall, gregarious, long-billed wader

WV

PLUMAGE Grey-brown above, mottled darker; **in flight, lacks wing-bars; white on lower back, rump;** tail closely barred black and white; long beak; shorter on legs than Black-tailed. **Brdg Male:** (early-Apr) Deep reddish-chestnut below.

HABITS More often on tidal creeks, estuaries; often also with Black-tailed on inland (brackish) waters. **Call:** Occ a *kwirrk* in flight.

Uran 1,2
Thane Crk
Sewri Bay
Elephanta
Coast-N,S
Fairly common

COMMON REDSHANK *Tringa totatus*

11"

Largish
wader with
orange-red legs

WV

♪

Most sites
occ Juhu airfield
Common

PLUMAGE Grey-brown above, lightly-scalloped; **diagnostic orange-red legs**; in flight, **extensive white on lower back, rump; broad, white trailing-edge of wings**. BRDG: (c. mid-Apr) Richer-brown above, mottled black and fulvous; more profusely marked below; brighter legs.

HABITS Marshes, reservoirs, canals, creeks, often several around with other waders; usually quite wary. Call: Loud, tuneful *tleu-he-hew*; more shrill than Greenshank's; calls chiefly in low flight; also an occ *tcheo* cry.

COMMON GREENSHANK *Tringa nebularia*

13"

Large,
grey-brown
wader with
greenish legs

WV

♪

Uran 1,2
Sewri Bay
Thane Crk
Manori Crk
Elephanta
Coast-N,S
Fairly common

PLUMAGE Grey-brown above, lightly-mottled; lightly-streaked neck, breast; **in flight, white lower-back, rump; no wing-bar; long, greenish legs** and faintly upturned, dark beak.

HABITS Inland and coastal wetlands; solitary or few around; **shy and wary**. Call: Melodious, ringing *teeu-tewtew* in low flight; less shrill and lower-pitched than Redshank's.

RELATED MARSH SANDPIPER *T stagnatilis* Smaller, slimmer; occ sharp *tcheuk* call, softer, less ringing than Greenshank's. Uncommon.

WOOD SANDPIPER *Tringa glareola*

8"

Slender, noisy wader with speckled plumage

WV

♪

PLUMAGE Brownish above, speckled paler; **whitish supercilium; in flight, white rump. Legs olive-green or yellowish-olive.** BRDG: (end-Apr) Brighter overall; richly-streaked breast.

HABITS Inland and coastal wetlands; usually several around, by themselves or with other waders; keeps to marsh-edges, low, damp grass; active and busy. Call: Generally noisy; sharp, mellow *tlui*; when flushed, a shrill *tsiff-siff*; rapidly-uttered notes roll into one another.

Uran 1,2
All creeks
MB marshes
Lakes 1,3
Fairly common

GREEN SANDPIPER *Tringa ochropus*

9"

Stoutish, dark-plumaged wader, often on inland waters

WV

●

PLUMAGE Very dark-brown above; **white below, streaked on neck, breast-sides; in flight, dark body, unmarked wings contrast with** pure white rump, tail; dark undersides of wings (pale-buff in Wood). Stouter build than Wood's.

HABITS Usually freshwater marshes; also forest pools, stream-banks; normally solitary; infrequently with other waders; shy, wary; moves rapidly at edge of water; **rises quickly in rapid flight.** Call: **Diagnostic, rapid, ringing** *tweet-tlui-twee* or *tweet-tlooeet-tlooet*; calls chiefly when flushed.

Uran 1,2
MB marshes
Lakes 1-3
Juhu airfield
also SGNP
Fairly common

COMMON SANDPIPER *Actitis hypoleucos*

8"

Frequently bobbing, small wader at edge of water

WV

Most sites
Fairly common

PLUMAGE Pale olive-brown above; paler about head, neck; whitish below, streaked on neck, breast-sides; **in flight, dark rump**, white sides to tail, narrow **white wing-bar**. **BRDG:** (mid-Apr) Deeper brown above, speckled darker; bolder markings on breast.

HABITS Inland and coastal wetlands; solitary or couple at edge of water; **constantly bobs head and tail**; flies low, a few rapid wing-beats followed by short glide. Call: Shrill, twittering *twee-tsee-tsi*, usually when flushed.

TEREK SANDPIPER *Xenus cinereus*

9"

Pale-coloured, slender wader with orange-yellow legs

WV

Uran 2
Thane Crk
Sewri Bay
Elephanta
Manori Crk
Coast-N,S
Uncommon

PLUMAGE Grey-brown above; paler face; white below, faintly streaked about breast; in flight, **white trailing-edges of wings, brownish rump; diagnostic long, upturned beak and orange-yellow legs**.

HABITS Chiefly coastal; sandy, rocky coasts, creeks; few scattered over an area; actively amid other waders; probes with upturned beak; has peculiar bobbing action. Call: Fairly vocal; soft fluty notes, chiefly in low flight but also on ground.

LITTLE STINT *Calidris minuta*

6"

Tiny, gregarious wader

WV

PLUMAGE Grey-brown above, mottled paler; **in flight, narrow, white wing-bar; grey-brown outertail feathers** and white sides to rump. **Black legs.** BRDG: (mid/late-Apr) Rufous-brown above, brightly-mottled; faint-rufous wash on fore-neck, breast.

Uran 1,2
Thane Crk
Manori Crk
Sewri Bay
Coast-N,S
Common

HABITS Inland and coastal (brackish) wetlands; quite gregarious, often many with other waders; **appears busy, dashing about**; strong, zig-zag flight. Call: Sharp *trri-trit-tit*, usually in flight; sounds like garbled trill when many call in chorus.

TEMMINCK'S STINT *Calidris temminckii*

6"

Tiny, gregarious wader

WV

PLUMAGE Pale grey-brown above, lightly marked; in flight, narrow white wing-bar and **diagnostic, white outertail feathers; dull-olive or olive-yellow legs.** BRDG: (mid-Apr) Warmer, richer-coloured above, mottled blackish; less rufous.

Uran 1,2
Sewri Bay
Thane Crk
Manori Crk
Dharamtar Crk
Coast-N,S
Fairly common

HABITS Same as Little, with which it is often seen. Call: Short twittering notes.

CURLEW SANDPIPER *Calidris ferruginea*

8"

Gregarious wader with gently decurved beak

WV

Coast-N,S
Uran 1,2
Thane Crk
Sewri Bay
Manori Crk
Fairly common

PLUMAGE Mottled grey-brown above; paler head; finely-streaked breast; in flight, **diagnostic white rump, wing-bar**. BRDG: Rufous and brick-red in plumage.

HABITS Coastal wetlands, lagoons; also inland marshes; gregarious, often with other waders. Call: Distinct, mellow *tchrrip* but not easily discernible in mixed flocks.

RELATED DUNLIN *C alpina* Less-curved beak and shorter on legs; **white sides of rump**. BRDG: Black centre of belly, abdomen. Fairly common.

RUFF *Philomachus pugnax*

11"

Variably-plumaged, fairly gregarious wader. Sexes differ

WV

Uran 1,2
Thane Crk
Sewri Bay
Naigon-Bassein
Coast-N,S
Fairly common

PLUMAGE Ashy-brown above, **conspicuously scaly-patterned**; paler below; in flight, dark rump, tail with **white on either side, narrow wing-bar**. Legs dull-green, orangish or yellowish-brown. Brdg Male: Variable – black, buff, chestnut, white; in winter, scaly-pattern, shorter beak, flight plumage and call-notes help distinguish from Redshank, especially when Ruff has orangish legs.

HABITS Inland and tidal wetlands; usually gregarious. Call: Occ soft *ptu-whut* when flushed; less vocal than most other waders.

BLACK-WINGED STILT *Himantopus himantopus*

15"

Very long-legged, black and white wader

R/LM/WV

♪

PLUMAGE White head, neck; glossy-black mantle, wings; white below; **diagnostic in flight**. Long straight beak, **reddish-pink legs**. Female: **More dark-brown where male is black.**

HABITS Inland and coastal wetlands; quite gregarious (large gatherings at Uran); often with other waders; always in and around water, often wading deep; peculiar, high-stepping walk. Call: Noisy; sharp *kik-kik* call on ground and in flight; also a shrill, piping alarm-note.

Uran 1,2
Thane Crk
Lakes 3
Fairly common
(very few breed)

PIED AVOCET *Recurvirostra avosetta*

15-17"

Lively, large, black and white wader with peculiarly upturned beak

WV

PLUMAGE **Pied**, at rest and in flight; black cap, black and white wings, mantle; **diagnostic long, black beak strikingly upturned**; blue-grey legs. Juv: Mottled pale-brown on back and wings.

HABITS Chiefly brackish, coastal wetlands, lagoons; usually small gatherings (however up to 250 sighted at Uran); often with godwits, redshanks, stilts; active, wades deep in water; occ up-ends duck-like; sweeps beak to pick tiny marine creatures. Call: Sharp, fluty *klueet*, in flight and on ground; occ a sharp *ptick-ptick*.

Uran 2
Thane Crk
Sewri Bay
Coast-N
Uncommon

SNIPES

WV *Highly cryptic-plumaged, tight-sitting, secretive birds of marshy cover; best seen when flushed; rarely emerge in open; not easy to identify with certainty in field. All except Jack Snipe are 10-11" (Jack is smaller, 7-8"). All are winter visitors; exact status not very clear but evidence of decline in numbers in recent times. Species sighted and/or reported here are:*

COMMON SNIPE *Gallinago gallinago* Conspicuous **white trailing-edge to wings**; whitish bands on underwings; may show pale-whitish towards tail-tip; crown-stripe; explosive, fast, usually zigzag flight with hoarse cry; sighted Uran, Dombivli.

PINTAIL SNIPE *G stenura* No white trailing-edge to flight-feathers; has crown-stripe; tail doesn't project beyond closed wings at rest; appears to be commoner snipe; sighted Uran, Vihar & Powai Lakes, Mira-Bhayander marshes, Manor area.

WOOD SNIPE *G nemoricola* Marginally larger; **darker mantle, scapulars**, with buff stripes; paler-buff stripes on head; known to rise with a hoarse call-note; several old records; unconfirmed sighting on Vihar Lake margins.

JACK SNIPE *Lymnocryptes minimus* **Smallest snipe** 7-8"; no white on pointed tail; lacks crown-stripe; extremely difficult to observe and flush; slower, usually straight flight, quickly dropping into cover; sighted once MB marshes; reported Uran.

BLACK-HEADED GULL *Larus ridibundus*

16"

Gregarious
coastal bird

WV

PLUMAGE Grey-white overall; **small, black ear-patches; white leading-edge of wings**, narrow black wing-tips. **BRDG:** Blackish-brown head. Juv: mottled grey-brown; dark sub-terminal tail-band.

Most sites
Common

HABITS Sociable; often scavenges; more agile than larger gulls. Call: Noisy; common call a loud, harsh, *khrreah* or *khwarr* scream.

RELATED **SLENDER-BILLED GULL** *L genei* On close sighting, longer neck, beak, gentler forehead-slope; small flocks sighted Uran, Thane Crk; often overlooked. Uncommon. *See inset*

BROWN-HEADED GULL *Larus brunnicephalus*

18"

Grey-white gull
with white in
wing-tips

WV

PLUMAGE Pale grey-white above; may have grey-brown patch behind eye; reddish beak, legs; in flight, **diagnostic white mirrors at tip of black primaries**. **BRDG:** (early/mid-Apr) Dull choco-brown head. Juv: Mottled brown and white; sub-terminal tail-band; extensive black wing-tips.

Coast-N,S
Uran 1,2
Elephanta
Sewri Bay
All creeks
Fairly common

HABITS Coastal and inland marshes, lakes; less gregarious than Black-headed; often by itself; **scavenges with kites and crows in harbour.** Call: Occ harsh *khraek* in flight.

22-23" HEUGLIN'S GULL *Larus heuglini*

Large, slaty-grey and white waterside bird
WV

Uran 1,2
Thane Crk
Sewri Bay
Elephanta
Coast-N,S
Uncommon

PLUMAGE Slaty-grey mantle, upperwings; **white head, streaked brownish** (white in brdg); white underbody, tail; **yellow legs, feet;** in flight, **darker-grey wings** with black wing-tips; small white mirrors. **Bright-yellow beak with red spot on lower-mandible.**

HABITS Usually small gatherings, often amid other waterside birds; leisurely flight. Call: A strident, fairly loud *kleeou*, almost exultant in tone.

26" PALLAS'S GULL *Larus ichthyaetus*

(inset) Very large grey and white gull
WV

Coast-N,S
Sewri Bay
Elephanta
Thane Crk
Uncommon

PLUMAGE Pale-grey mantle, wings; **white head with black around eyes**, occ streaked; **in flight, prominent white flash on outer wings;** slight black tips to flight-feathers; **large, yellow beak with dark band towards tip.** BRDG: (seen early-Mar) Black head with white around eyes; red patch towards tip of beak.

HABITS Often solitary; occ up to 6 around. More often on coast.

22" YELLOW-LEGGED GULL *Larus cachinnans*

Large, pale-grey and white waterside bird
WV

Uran 1,2
Sewri Bay
Thane Crk
Coast-N,S
Uncommon

PLUMAGE Paler-grey mantle, upperwings than Heuglin's; whitish head, variably streaked darker; black tips to flight-feathers with less white (smaller mirrors) towards wing-tips.

HABITS Often several around; seen with crows and kites at fishing sites; usually scavenges. Call: Deep, hoarse *khee-yow*.

WHISKERED TERN *Chlidonias hybridus*

10"

Silvery-grey and white tern with slightly-forked tail

WV

PLUMAGE Uniform pale-grey above; some black on crown, band from eye to nape; in flight, **slight fork to short, grey tail.** Beak dark-reddish in summer, almost blackish during winter. **BRDG:** (end-Apr) Jet-black crown; **white cheeks (whiskers), neck-sides; dark-grey below, blacker toward abdomen.**

Most sites
Fairly common

HABITS Mostly inland wetlands; sparingly on coast; flies 5-8 m from surface; plunges for food. Call: Shrill *kyeeak*, typically in flight.

LITTLE TERN *Sterna albifrons*

9"

Small, lively tern with narrow wings and yellow legs

R/LM

PLUMAGE Pale grey-white above; **black on nape;** blackish beak. **BRDG:** (mid-Mar-Jul) **White forehead, black crown, eye-stripe; yellow beak, tipped black.** Juv: Lightly mottled with dark on back.

Uran 2
Elephanta
Coast-N,S
Mumbai coast
Thane Crk
Manori Crk
Fairly common

Small nos known to nest on islets off Uttan-Gorai coast till early-1990s

HABITS Coastal and inland wetlands; quite sociable and energetic; flies low with quick wing beats; occ hovers like Pied Kingfisher before plunging for food. Call: Sharp *kree-eik* in low flight; occ a chattering *keer-keerri*.

GULL-BILLED TERN *Gelochelidon nilotica*

15"

Pale-grey, heavy-bodied tern with stout, black beak

WV

Most coastal sites occ inland waters
Fairly common

PLUMAGE Pale-grey above; whiter head, streaked black towards nape; black patch behind eyes; white below; **greyer tail with shallow fork** (deeper than Whiskered's); **black legs, stout, short, beak.** BRDG: (Apr) Jet-black cap.

HABITS Solitary or 3-4 around; doesn't plunge often; occ hawks insects 5-8 m above ground. Call: Occ a hoarse *khwuekk*.

RELATED SANDWICH TERN *S sandvicensis* Larger, longer, slimmer black beak, usually tipped yellow; more black on crown/nape (slight crest). Scarce.

CASPIAN TERN *Sterna caspia*

20"

Large tern with prominent coral-red beak

WV

Uran 1,2
Thane Crk
Coast-N,S
Uncommon

Much declined on Mumbai coast

PLUMAGE Pale-grey above; **dark-streaked forehead, crown**; white below; **diagnostic heavy, coral-red beak, black legs; in OH flight, short tail with shallow fork,** white body and **darker flight-feathers.** BRDG: (mid-Apr) Jet-black cap. Juv: Mottled brown above.

HABITS Chiefly coastal wetlands; occ inland; solitary or 3-4 birds; less agile than the smaller terns; hovers and plunges down; often settles on sandy patches with other terns, gulls. Call: Distinctive loud, rasping *kreaaha* in flight.

GREAT CRESTED TERN *Sterna bergii*

20"

Large, dark-grey tern with yellow-green beak

WV

PLUMAGE White head, neck; **black-speckled crown, nuchal crest**; dark tips to flight-feathers; conspicuous **large yellow-green beak**. **BRDG:** (early-Apr) Glossy, **jet-black crown**, nape and **nuchal crest**; white forehead, lores; deeper-grey mantle contrasts with white neck; white below.

Coast-N,S
Uran 2
Scarce

Thrice sighted 2000-2001 winter

HABITS Often on sea; occ coastal areas, tidal creeks (sighted Revdanda); solitary or 3-4 around; flies 5-10 m above waters, scanning below, momentarily hovering before plunging. **Call:** Occ loud, rasping *chrrrak* in low flight (heard Uran).

BLACK-BELLIED TERN *Sterna acuticauda*

12-14"

Tern with deeply-forked tail and orangish beak

WV

PLUMAGE Pale-grey above; streaked crown; black patch behind eyes; white below, with greyish wash about fore-neck, breast; **yellowish-orange beak**; **pale-orange legs**. Deeply-forked tail, brighter, orangish-red beak help separate from commoner Whiskered. **BRDG:** Glossy-black crown; grey breast, **black below**; white sides of face, chin, throat.

Uran 2
Lakes 1,3
Coast-S
Uncommon

HABITS Chiefly inland tern; small parties along rivers, lakes, marshes; usually flies low; fast and active. **Call:** In flight, a high-pitched *khraek* or *krrek* cry.

PIED KINGFISHER *Ceryle rudis*

12"

Active, black and white bird around fresh water

R/LM

♪

Lakes 3
Tansa Lk
Vaitarna Lk
Manori Crk
Thane Crk
Powai Lk (once)

Uncommon

PLUMAGE Speckled, pied; **black head, crest,** finely-streaked white; long, white supercilium; broad, **black band through eyes**; white below, with **two black bands across breast.** Female: Single incomplete gorget.

HABITS Rivers, lakes, occ creeks; pairs usually close by; active, frequently hovers in flight, 5-8 m high; perches on tree-stumps, rocks, poles. Call: Distinctive, sharp, twittering *chrrr-ruk-cherruk,* chiefly in flight.

COMMON KINGFISHER *Alcedo atthis*

6"

Stumpy-tailed, blue and chestnut bird

R

♪ ● ●

All sites
Common

Sighted S Mumbai, incl attending a fish-tank on the 10th flr of a skyscraper

PLUMAGE Iridescent-blue above, with variable greenish wash; at close range, blackish barring seen on crown; **rufous-chestnut cheeks, underbody**; white chin, throat, small patch on neck-sides; **coral-red legs.**

HABITS Streams, lakes, marshes; occ tidal creeks; solitary or pairs; darts low over water; hovers, dives upon sighting fish; also catches tadpoles, aquatic insects. Call: A shrill *chee* and *chichee*, mostly during low flight over water; occ a short trilling song when brdg (Mar-Jun).

WHITE-THROATED KINGFISHER *Halcyon smyrnensis*

11"

Familiar bright-blue bird with white throat

R

All sites
Common

PLUMAGE Bright-turquoise above; **chestnut-brown head, neck; diagnostic white throat, centre of breast**; chestnut-brown below; in flight, **white wing-patch. Coral-red beak, legs.**

HABITS Inland and coastal wetlands; often away from water, even in urban areas; solitary or pairs; catches insects, lizards, occ fish. **Call: Diagnostic loud scream**; trilling *kileelililili* song Mar-May (brdg); sporadically sings other times of year.

BLACK-CAPPED KINGFISHER *Halcyon pileata*

12"

Purplish-blue kingfisher with white collar

LM

PLUMAGE Diagnostic black cap; white neck-collar; purplish-blue mantle, wings; black shoulder-patches; white throat, upper-breast; pale tawny-rufous below; in flight, conspicuous **white and black on wings. Bright-red beak.**

Coast-N,S
Thane Crk
Manori Crk
Sewri Bay
Uncommon

HABITS Strictly coastal bird; solitary or pairs; settles on fishing poles, boats, floats.
Call: Occ cackling scream, shriller than White-throated's; mainly in flight.

WIRE-TAILED SWALLOW *Hirundo smithii*

5-6" + c. 6" tail

Steel-blue and white bird with long outertail feathers

LM/WV

Uran 1,2
Lakes 1-3
Most creeks
RFM
Uncommon

PLUMAGE Metallic-blue above; chestnut crown; **diagnostic pure-white below**; wire-like streamers on outertail feathers (shorter in female).

HABITS Inland marshes, lakes; occ creeks; small gatherings; roosts in reed beds, mangroves. Call: Pleasant, twittering *chrr-chit* in flight; brdg male has twittering song.

RELATED STREAK-THROATED SWALLOW *H fluvicola* **5" WV/R** Shorter, slightly-forked tail; chestnut crown; streaked throat, breast; sighted MB marshes, Uran, Panvel, Lonavla, Malshej. Uncommon.

CLAMOROUS REED WARBLER *Acrocephalus stentoreus*

7"

Noisy, brownish bird of reed beds and mangrove

R

♪

Thane Crk
Manori Crk
Malad Crk
Bassein Crk
Dharamtar Crk
Uran 2
MB marshes
Uncommon

PLUMAGE Brown above, with slight olivish wash; **pale-buff supercilium**, underbody; tawny toward flanks; **salmon coloured inside of mouth**.

HABITS More common in mangrove creeks; solitary or few around; difficult to spot; occ clambers into view. Call: **Diagnostic loud, grating, rambling notes**; most vocal May-Sep.

Clamorous highly vulnerable to pressures on mangrove habitat

RELATED BLYTH'S REED WARBLER *A dumetorum* **5" WV** Paler grey-brown above, also with olivish wash; fairly common; largely forest-edge, scrub, cultivation; occ suburban parks. Common.

YELLOW WAGTAIL *Motacilla flava*

7"

Slender, long-tailed, ground bird with yellow underbody

WV

PLUMAGE Dull olive-brown above, occ with faint yellow-green tinge; variable slaty-grey crown; stripe over eye; dark tail has whitish outer feathers; **whitish chin, throat merges into pale-yellow below.**

Most sites
Common

In recent years quite abundant on landfill sites – Gorai, Deonar

HABITS Around damp, grassy areas, cultivation; also grazing cattle; active and sociable; restless; great congregations roost in reed beds (Talzan, MB marshes, Uran), mangrove creeks or feed on landfill sites. **Call:** High-pitched *tchiss-tzit*, occ sprinkled with harsher *tscirrr*.

CITRINE WAGTAIL *Motacilla citreola*

7"

Slender, greyish wagtail with yellow about face

WV

PLUMAGE Pale-greyish above; darker wings with conspicuous white wing-bars; **diagnostic slight yellow on forehead, broad supercilium;** yellowish throat, upper-breast, fading into dull-white below. **BRDG: Bright-yellow head**, blackish or deep-grey back on arrival (late-Sep/early-Oct) and occ early-summer (late-Mar). *See inset*

Uran 1,2
All creeks
Lakes 2
Coast-N,S
Uncommon

HABITS Primarily damp grasslands, marsh-edges; small nos often with other wagtails. **Call:** Wheezy *tzaep* or *tzeesp*.

GREY WAGTAIL *Motacilla cinerea*

7"

Conspicuously long-tailed, grey and yellow wagtail

WV

● ● ●

Uran 1,2
Lakes 1-3
All creeks
forest streams
occ S Mumbai
Common

PLUMAGE Distinctly grey above (can appear blue-grey); **yellow-green rump**; pale-white supercilium; **long, black tail** with white outer feathers; whitish chin, throat; variable sulphur-yellow below. Brdg Male: **(late-Sep or early-Apr) Diagnostic black chin, throat**; bright-yellow below. Brdg Female: Pale-yellow below; lacks black chin, throat.

HABITS Open, damp areas, along forest streams; solitary or pairs, seldom gregarious, except at landfill sites; wags tail. Call: Shrill *tszeet* or *tis-zeet* mostly in flight, when taking off or in low flight.

WHITE WAGTAIL *Motacilla alba*

7"

Slender, black and white wagtail

WV

Uran 1,2
Lakes 1-3
All creeks
RFM
occ S, suburban Mumbai
Uncommon

PLUMAGE Diagnostic white forehead, ear-coverts; black top of head, nape; **grey back**; black wings have white bands; black tail with white outer feathers; **white throat; diagnostic black bib**; white below.

HABITS Open, damp areas, wetland margins; also open grounds, canals; sometimes with other wagtails, solitary or pairs. Call: A lively, sharp *tchiszeek* sometimes interspersed with slightly-grating *tcheek*.

WHITE-BROWED WAGTAIL *Motacilla maderaspatensis*

8"

Black and white wagtail with conspicuous white supercilium

R/LM

PLUMAGE Diagnostic, **long white supercilium**; jet-black above; broad **white band on black wings**; black tail with white outer-feathers; **jet-black throat, breast**; white below. Female: Similar but deep ashy-brown where male is black.

HABITS Fresh-water streams, rivers, ponds; solitary or pairs; occ family parties (seen Jun-Sep); perches on rocks, poles; jerky, low flight. Call: Shrill *tszi-szit* usually in flight; brdg male (Mar-Jul) has musical song of several notes; snatches of song intermittently other months.

Alibaug-Murud Lakes 3
Tansa
Vaitarna
also Shyd
Uncommon

BLACK-BREASTED WEAVER *Ploceus benghalensis*

6"

Black-breasted weaver of reed-covered marshes

R/LM

PLUMAGE Brdg Male: **Bright-yellow crown**; streaked fulvous and blackish above; dull-white below; **diagnostic broad, blackish-brown band across breast**. Female: Streaked fulvous and blackish above; dull-yellow supercilium.

HABITS Reed-covered marshes; small parties first noted at Uran Aug-Sep 2002, when several nests found. Call: Distinctive wheezy, whistling calls around nesting sites; also a sharp but low *sik* or *tseec-tseec* call of male.

Uran 1,2

Also sighted along NH-8, c. 20 km N of Mumbai

FORESTS

Dry and mixed-deciduous, semi-evergreen and evergreen forests in N Konkan, along hill-slopes, and Sahyadri. Some species may also be seen at forest-edges and in urban parks.

Elephanta
Jawahar (Wada-Kasa-Jawahar-Mokhada-Khodala-Suriamal)
KBS (Karnala Bird Sanctuary)
Kohoj (incl Takmak)
Matheran (Matheran Range, Prabalgadh)
MNP (Maharashtra Nature Park)
S&C Mumbai (Navy Nagar, Malabar Hill, Jijamata Udyan)
Murbad (incl base of Malshej Ghat/Nane Ghat, Barvi-Murbad Rd)
Phansad (Phansad Wildlife Sanctuary)
Sajanpada (incl forests along low ridges west of NH-8)
SGNP (Sanjay Gandhi National Park: incl Nagla Block)
Shyd (Sahyadri: Bhimashankar, Mahabaleshwar, Lonavala-Khandala, Malshej Ghat, Naneghat, Karjat and Khopoli areas)
Tansa (Tansa Wildlife Sanctuary)
Tungar (Tungareshwar Wildlife Sanctuary: incl all trails, Chinchoti)

WHITE-EYED BUZZARD *Butastur teesa*

17"

Crow-size pale-brown raptor of light forest

WV

PLUMAGE Ashy-brown above; whitish nape-patch; **white throat; whitish eyes**; dark gular stripe; **pale-buff below, barred darker**; rufous-brown tail; **pale shoulder-patch in flight; in OH flight, pale underwings**; variable rufous on wing-coverts. Juv: Brownish eyes.

HABITS Sometimes open areas; solitary or scattered pairs; leisurely flight; regularly soars; sometimes descends to ground. Call: 2-noted *tchi-tchweeer* **mewing cry**, the second note long-drawn.

SGNP
Kohoj
Sajanpada
Shyd
Elephanta
Murbad
occ S&C Mumbai
Uncommon

ORIENTAL HONEY-BUZZARD *Pernis ptilorhyncus*

26-27"

Slender-headed raptor

R/LM

PLUMAGE Chiefly dark-brown above; head brown or buff-grey; **short nuchal crest; pale-brown below, usually streaked/mottled** darker; in **OH flight**, long, broad wings held flat; **pale flight-feathers, dark-banded** across length; longish **tail has dark and pale bands**.

HABITS Occ cultivation; often solitary; leisurely flight over forest, around cliffs; feeds on honey, bee-larvae, rodents, small birds. Call: High-pitched, whistling *wheeeeuu*, both on perch and in flight; occ calls during night.

SGNP
Tungar
Phansad
KBS
Shyd
Jawahar
Tansa
Uncommon

Sighted carrying nesting material SGNP, Phansad

SHIKRA *Accipiter badius*

12-14"

Small, long-tailed, hawk

R/LM

● ●

Most sites
occ S Mumbai
Fairly common

PLUMAGE Ashy-grey above; **golden-yellow eyes;** dull-white below, **finely barred rufous on breast,** partly on belly; greyish gular (not always visible); in OH flight, **dark-banded tail;** pale underwings, barred mostly on flight-feathers. Female: Browner above. Juv: Streaked below; more marked underwings and tail.

HABITS Solitary or pairs; keeps to leafy branches; occ descends to drink; soars on thermals, rising high. **Call:** Loud *tchi-tchew*, scolding tone like Black Drongo's, but much higher pitch; most vocal Feb-Apr (brdg).

BLACK EAGLE *Ictinaetus malayensis*

28-31"

Large, broad-winged, blackish raptor

R/LM

Shyd
Matheran
SGNP
KBS
Phansad
Uncommon

PLUMAGE Deep blackish-brown overall; in OH flight, **dark plumage,** yellow legs, long, broad wings with **widely-splayed primaries;** variable greyish barring on tail; in flight, **broad wings held in 'V'** with upturned primaries. Juv: Pale-brown above, palest about head, neck; broadly marked dark on pale underbody.

HABITS Chiefly hill-forest; often solitary; glides across forested valleys or low over forest canopy; feeds on birds, their eggs, rodents, lizards. **Call:** Occ high-pitched scream; shrill cries heard during brdg display (Dec-Feb, Mhblswr, Bhmshnkr).

CRESTED SERPENT EAGLE *Spilornis cheela*

27-29"

Large, conspicuously-barred, dark-brown raptor

R

♪

PLUMAGE Dark-brown above; **roundish, brown and white nuchal crest, partly erectile;** yellow cere, lores and legs; pale-brown below, marked white and black; **in OH flight, banded underwings, tail.**

HABITS Usually pairs, circling over forest, calling often; rests in leafy branches; soars regularly; occ wanders over cultivation. **Call:** Diagnostic, **loud, whistling** *ptuwheeee-pteu-pteu* or *kueeee-kee-ke* in flight, first note longer; variations of this call, sometimes only first note; rarely calls on perch.

Tungar
SGNP
KBS
Phansad
Elephanta
Shyd
Jawahar
Tansa
Fairly common

CHANGEABLE HAWK EAGLE *Spizaetus cirrhatus*

27-29"

A slender, crested raptor with banded wings and tail

R/LM

PLUMAGE Brownish above; **diagnostic dark crest;** whitish below, **streaked darker on throat, breast,** in OH flight, longish, banded tail, rounded wings, streaked underbody, **darkest about flanks,** undertail-coverts. **Juv:** Paler, almost whitish head.

HABITS Perches upright on tall forest tree or flies over forest; occ around habitation; solitary or pairs. **Call:** High-pitched, **loud scream in crescendo;** also calls in flight.

SGNP
Phansad
Tansa
Bhmshnkr
Shyd
Scarce

SHAHEEN FALCON *Falco peregrinus (peregrinator)*

16-18"
Broad-
shouldered,
pointed-winged
raptor
R/LM

PLUMAGE (resident race): Deep slaty-grey above; **blackish head, moustachial stripes** (appear like hood); **diagnostic rufous below**, barred darker below breast; in OH flight, lightly-marked flight-feathers, **rufous underbody**.
Juv: Dark-brown above; boldly-streaked below.

● ●

Shyd (breeds)
SGNP
KBS
Kohoj
Tungar
S Mumbai (rains)
Fairly common

HABITS Largely cliff-sides in forested country; pairs often close by; swift flight, **hurtling at tremendous speed**; strikes prey in mid-air; has select feeding spots. Call: Shrill *chirrrrr* scream, normally in fast flight; occ a sharp *kek-kekeke* cry.

RELATED PEREGRINE FALCON *F p calidus* WV Slaty-grey above (**paler than Shaheen**); broad black moustachial stripes; **whitish below, barred darker below breast**; coast, marshes; also urban areas. Uncommon. *See centre inset*

EURASIAN HOBBY *F subbuteo* **12-14"** WV Slaty-grey above; almost blackish head, moustachial stripes; white cheeks, throat; broadly-streaked dark below; **diagnostic, deep-rufous thighs, undertail-coverts; in OH flight**, profusely-marked underbody, wings. Sighted SGNP, Tansa. Uncommon. *See below*

GREY JUNGLEFOWL *Gallus sonneratii*

Male 27-30"
Female 17"

Greyish,
domestic
fowl-like bird.
Sexes differ

R

SGNP
KBS
Tungar
Phansad
Shyd
Matheran
Kohoj
Uncommon

PLUMAGE Deep-grey above, with **white shaft-streaks**; **waxy-yellowish spots on head, upper back**; purple-black gloss on wings and **long, arching tail**; dark-grey below, with broad, white streaks on breast; **crimson comb, face and wattles.** Female: Dark-brown above, finely-mottled buff and white; **whitish below, broadly marked darker on breast.**

HABITS Pairs or small gatherings; rummages amid leaf-litter; wary, runs for cover on slightest alarm. Call: **Diagnostic cock's loud crow**, most familiar bird-call of forest; various cackling notes.

RED SPURFOWL *Galloperdix spadicea*

14"

Dark, skulking,
hen-like bird
of forest floor

R

SGNP
Phansad
Tungar
Shyd
Sajanpada
KBS
Fairly common

PLUMAGE Dull rufous-brown overall, marked buff and grey (pale edging to feathers); **greyish face, neck; bare, brick-red patch around eyes. Reddish legs with spurs.** Female: Mottled-darker above; more scalloped below.

HABITS Pairs or small bands (occ family parties) in **stony, overgrown terrain**; wary, scampers into cover; emerges in clearings, forest roads; usually flies only when flushed; roosts in trees. Call: Cock's crow, rather quarrelsome in tone, a harsh *khrr-khrr-kwaek*; other chuckling notes.

COMMON PEAFOWL *Pavo cristatus*

Male 80-90"
Female 36-38"

Brilliantly-plumaged familiar ground bird. Sexes differ

R

♪

SGNP
Phansad
Tansa
KBS
Shyd
Uncommon

A few birds survive Malabar Hill

PLUMAGE Brilliant-blue neck, breast; long, bronze-green train, profusely marked with richly-coloured eye-spots; **fan-shaped crest of wire-like feathers; chestnut in wings.** Female: Smaller; **lacks long train; has pale-white face-sides, throat;** metallic-green on neck.

HABITS Wary and alert; solitary males or small, mixed parties; runs into cover upon alarm; roosts in trees. Call: Loud, familiar *mae-ow* call of male; most vocal mid-May-Sep (brdg); also nasal alarm-notes and a loud, 1-note crow.

YELLOW-FOOTED GREEN PIGEON *Treron phoenicoptera*

13"

Stout, olive-green forest pigeon

R

♪

SGNP
Phansad
Tungar
KBS
Shyd
occ MNP
also occ Aarey,
Alibaug
Fairly common

PLUMAGE Olive-green above, with slight yellow wash; ashy-grey head; **olive-yellow collar;** dull-lilac shoulder-patch (faint in female); blackish wings with yellow band; **yellow below,** greener towards abdomen; **diagnostic yellow legs.**

HABITS Arboreal; usually small bands; up to 20 sighted SGNP; strong flier; often with other frugivorous birds. Call: Distinctive musical, whistling of 6-20 notes, rambling in tone; mellow but quite far-reaching.

POMPADOUR GREEN PIGEON *Treron pompadora*

11"

Red-legged forest pigeon. Sexes differ

R

PLUMAGE **Chestnut-maroon mantle**; greyish crown, nape; **black and yellow in wings**; yellowish-green below, with **variable, faint-orangish wash on breast** (in good light); **reddish-brown undertail-coverts** (seen from below). Female: **Lacks chestnut-maroon mantle**, orange tinge on breast.

HABITS Arboreal, mostly leafy upper branches, usually pairs, on fruiting trees with other birds. Call: Musical, whistling notes, higher in tone than Yellow-footed's.

KBS
Phansad
Shyd
Matheran
occ Kohoj,
SGNP, Tungar
Uncommon

EMERALD DOVE *Chalcophaps indica*

11"

Deep-vinaceous and emerald-green forest dove

R

PLUMAGE Pale blue-grey crown, nape; **whitish forehead, supercilium**; vinous-red sides of face, continuous with underbody; **diagnostic emerald-green mantle**; bright-red beak. Pale-grey and black lower back. Female: Less grey, more vinous-red on crown.

HABITS Chiefly arboreal; occ gleans on forest tracts, clearings or visits water-holes; usually pairs; shy and wary; flies fast and low along paths. Call: **Distinctive soft *huoon* or *hoooun*; may call for several minutes, most vocal late-May-Aug (brdg).

SGNP
KBS
Phansad
Shyd
Matheran
Murbad
Jawahar
Uncommon

ORIENTAL TURTLE DOVE *Streptopelia orientalis*

13"

Stocky dove
with rufous-
scaled mantle

R (Shyd);
LM/WV
(N Konkan)

Shyd
Matheran
Phansad
KBS
Jawahar
Elephanta
occ SGNP,
Sajanpada
Uncommon

PLUMAGE Pale vinous-brown head, neck;
diagnostic, scaly-patterned mantle (dark
centred feathers, fringed with rufous); **black and
grey 'chess-board' patch on neck-sides; dark,
graduated tail, with pale-grey outer feathers;**
pale-vinous below, paler on abdomen.

HABITS Largely arboreal but also gleans on
ground; pairs or up to 5-7 birds; wary, taking to
cover on disturbance. Call: **Distinctive,
somewhat drowsy, grating** *ghur-kroo-ghu-grooo*,
normally 4-noted.

GREEN IMPERIAL PIGEON *Ducula aenea*

18"

Large, deep-
green and grey
forest pigeon

R/LM

Phansad
Shyd
occ Matheran,
Tungar, SGNP
Uncommon

PLUMAGE Pale-grey head, neck, continuous
with underbody; may show slight pinkish wash
(in good light); **coppery-gloss to metallic-green
mantle**, much of wings, uppertail; **maroon
undertail-coverts;** grey beak and pink-red legs.

HABITS Prefers tall forest; largely arboreal;
solitary, pairs or small bands; frugivorous, often
with other birds; strong flier; occ descends to
ground to drink. Call: **Distinctive, deep
chuckling of several notes** – *wuk-worr-worrr*,
notes rolling into one another.

MALABAR PARAKEET *Psittacula columboides*

15"

Blue-green, long-tailed forest bird

R/LM

PLUMAGE Pale bluish-green overall; fine black collar from chin around hind-neck, bordered by broader, bright blue-green band; **diagnostic blue wings and yellow-tipped, blue tail; largely reddish beak. Female: Blackish beak; lacks blue-green neck-band.**

Shyd
Phansad
KBS
Tansa
occ SGNP
Uncommon

HABITS Chiefly arboreal, keeping to tall trees; small bands; fast, swift flight; agile and noisy; often with other birds on fruiting, flowering trees; occ fields. **Call:** **Distinctive 2-noted** *tch-chwae*, the second note longer; calls mostly in flight.

PLUM-HEADED PARAKEET *Psittacula cyanocephala*

14"

Small, greenish parrot with colourful head. Sexes differ

R

PLUMAGE Bright grass-green. **Diagnostic reddish-plum head,** with bluish-violet wash on nape, crown; **maroon patch on wing-shoulder; white-tipped, bluish central tail-feathers. Female: Dull blue-grey head;** yellowish collar; indistinct maroon shoulder-patch. Yellowish beak.

SGNP
KBS
Phansad
Sajanpada
Jawahar
Shyd
Matheran
Fairly common

HABITS Largely arboreal; small, noisy flocks; visits fruiting, flowering trees; also forest-edge, cultivation; strong, fast flight. **Call:** **Diagnostic, loud, shrill** *tooi-tooi* usually in flight; has distinctly **interrogative** tone; soft, chattering notes on perch.

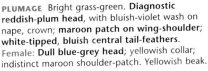

VERNAL HANGING PARAKEET *Loriculus vernalis*

6"

Small, lively, green
bird with very
short tail

R/LM

Phansad
KBS
Shyd
occ SGNP,
Tansa, Jawahar
Elephanta,
S Mumbai
also occ Aarey
Uncommon

PLUMAGE Bright grass-green; **diagnostic
crimson rump; very short tail; blue patch on
throat** (visible in good light); orangish-red beak.
Female: Lacks blue throat-patch.

HABITS Active and agile in canopy; usually
several around; occ solitary; often with other
small birds; acrobatic and inquisitive; not easily
observable; swift flight. **Call:** Fairly loud, sharp
chie-chee-chee in fast flight; occ calls in canopy.

COMMON HAWK CUCKOO *Hierococcyx varius*

13"

Broad-winged,
ashy-grey,
arboreal bird

BV (rains)

Most sites
also occ Aarey,
suburban
Mumbai
Fairly common

PLUMAGE Clear ashy-grey above; **long, black-
banded tail, tipped pale-rufous;** dingy-white
throat; **dull-rufous breast;** barred brown on
abdomen, flanks. **Juv:** Broadly-streaked below.

HABITS Arboreal, rarely descending into low
bush; mostly solitary; never easy to locate.
Call: Diagnostic; loud, clear *pee-pehea* or *wee-
peiwhit;* sounds like '*brain fever*' repeated several
times in crescendo to abruptly end; begins calling
late-Mar; most vocal May-Aug, frequently calling
in overcast weather; may call at night. Rarely
sighted Oct-Mar when silent.

INDIAN CUCKOO *Cuculus micropterus*

13"

Long-tailed, slaty-grey bird, conspicuously-barred below

BV (rains)

SGNP
KBS
Phansad
Shyd
Uncommon

PLUMAGE Slaty-grey above, with slight brownish wash; **paler-grey head, throat, upper-breast**; whitish below, **broadly barred blackish**; black sub-terminal tail-band, whitish on outer feathers. Female: Rufous-brown throat, upper-breast.

HABITS Arboreal; difficult to locate, even when calling. **Call: Diagnostic; fluty, 4-noted, clear** *ko-ko-tak-ko* without any pause between notes; last note lowest in scale, interpreted as *'crossword puzzle'*; occ a 3-noted call; calls through day in overcast weather, sometimes during night.

BANDED BAY CUCKOO *Cacomantis sonneratii*

10"

Slim, rufous-brown and white, barred bird

BV

SGNP
KBS
Tansa
Phansad
Matheran
Shyd
Elephanta
Sajanpada
Jawahar
Uncommon

PLUMAGE **Rufous-brown above, finely barred blackish**; rufous-tipped tail, barred; **white supercilium**, face, with dark patch around eyes; **whitish below, finely cross-barred brown**.

HABITS Chiefly arboreal; difficult to sight; mostly solitary; often overlooked; observed hunting insects in flycatcher manner.
Call: Diagnostic 4-noted *wee-tee-tei-teu* call from high perch; may call often in overcast weather; quite similar in tone to Indian Cuckoo but higher pitch; also known to have a longer call of several notes in crescendo.

GREY-BELLIED CUCKOO *Cacomantis passerinus*

9"

Slim, arboreal, greyish bird

BV

KBS
Phansad
Shyd
Kohoj
Jawahar
Uncommon

PLUMAGE Dark-grey overall, blackish on wing-tips; pale-grey and white towards abdomen. **Hepatic Female: Like Banded Bay**, but brighter rufous-chestnut; slight barring on crown; white supercilium indistinct or absent; unbarred tail.

HABITS Keeps to leafy, upper branches; usually solitary; quite active, hunting flycatcher-style; occ on overhead telegraph wire. Call: **Diagnostic, whistling, somewhat melancholic** *whi-tcheer*; also 4-noted *wheety-tchee-ti* in a high pitch; when brdg, several whistling notes in crescendo. Often calls in overcast weather, occ at night.

DRONGO CUCKOO *Surniculus lugubris*

10"

Long-tailed, black, drongo-like bird

BV

SGNP
Tansa
KBS
Shyd (rains)
also occ Gorai,
Aarey,
Datiwere-Kelve
Uncommon

PLUMAGE Glossy-black overall; seen from below, **variable white barring on undertail-coverts**; more slender beak and **shallower tail fork** distinguish from Black Drongo.

HABITS Arboreal; sometimes forest-edge, groves; often solitary; less active than Drongo; overlooked due to resemblance to Black Drongo; occ hunts flycatcher-style; cuckoo flight quite evident. Call: Diagnostic 5-7 noted, high-pitched, whistling *peee-peeee-pee-pee-pe-peea* call, quite musical in tone; calls in crescendo and ends abruptly.

COLLARED SCOPS OWL *Otus bakkamoena*

9"

Small, upright owl with conspicuous ear-tufts

R

SGNP
Phansad
Shyd
also occ Gorai
Uncommon

PLUMAGE Buff-brown above (can appear grey-brown), **profusely-mottled; diagnostic pale-buff hind-neck collar;** dull-white below, faintly-mottled darker; **conspicuous ear-tufts.** Eyes brown or yellowish-brown.

HABITS Difficult to sight; usually pairs; spends day in dense foliage or tree-cavity; starts moving around dusk. Call: **Distinctive, mellow, doleful** *whuu-t* or *whoo-k* with interrogative tone; far-reaching; calls every few seconds, often intermittently through night; more vocal Dec-Feb.

JUNGLE OWLET *Glaucidium radiatum*

8"

Distinctly-barred forest owl

R

Most sites
SGNP
Fairly common

PLUMAGE Brown above (varies from deep ashy-brown to choco-brown), richly close-barred; **barred wings; white chin, throat, abdomen-centre;** barred brown and buff-white below; **lemon-yellow eyes.**

HABITS Usually pairs, sometimes several in vicinity; rests in foliage or tree-cavity by day; most often sighted and heard owl during day. Call: **Diagnostic, loud, rambling whistle,** beginning with *koorrrr*, then *koorr-kuk-koo-kuk*; rises in tempo to abruptly end; familiar call of mixed-deciduous forest; also chattering notes.

BROWN HAWK OWL *Ninox scutulata*

12"

Dark-brown, hawk-like forest owl

R

♪

SGNP
Phansad
Tungar
KBS
Shyd
Uncommon

PLUMAGE Dark-brown above; slightly **paler forehead**; dark bands on pale-tipped tail; **dull-white breast, abdomen, heavily-streaked rich rufous-brown; bright golden-yellow eyes.**

HABITS Elusive; rarely sighted; usually pairs close by; keeps to secluded, leafy branches by day; hawk-like flight; usually emerges past sunset. **Call: Diagnostic, soft, tuneful, 2-noted** *oo-uk*; may call up to 12 times, repeating after slight pause; more vocal Feb-Jun (possibly brdg).

CRESTED TREESWIFT *Hemiprocne coronata*

8-9"

Slender, bluish-grey, fork-tailed bird

R/LM

KBS (nesting)
Phansad
Karjat
Khopoli
Murbad
also occ Aarey,
Gorai,
Navi Mumbai
Uncommon

PLUMAGE Pale blue-grey above; **dark crest, wings, long tail; chestnut face-sides**; ashy-grey upper-breast; whiter below. Long, deeply-forked tail extends beyond closed wings at rest. **Female:** Lacks chestnut on face-sides.

HABITS Pairs or small parties, hawking insects over forest and clearings; **wheeling, graceful flight**, slower than most other swifts; often settles on bare, upper branches (on which it nests); often overlooked. **Call:** Feeble 2-noted scream, *whe-chack*; occ a sharp *kea-kea* call; more vocal Mar-Jun (brdg).

MALABAR TROGON *Harpactes fasciatus*

12"

Long-tailed,
elusive forest bird.
Sexes differ

R

PLUMAGE Blackish head, upper-breast; deep-cinnamon (tawny) mantle, rump, black-tipped tail; **white in outertail feathers;** blackish wings with fine white barring; **white gorget** separates upper-breast from **pinkish-crimson underbody. Female: Deep-tawny head,** upper-breast; paler below.

HABITS Shy, rarely sighted bird; pairs usually close by; keeps to middle storey of dense forest; makes short sallies after insects. **Call: Distinctive mellow,** whistling *fue* or *pheu*, up to 8 times at a stretch, but typically 3-4; grating alarm-note.

SGNP
occ Shyd,
Tungar,
Phansad, KBS
Scarce

*Less than
six sightings
since 1978*

ORIENTAL DWARF KINGFISHER *Ceyx erithacus*

5"

Tiny, vividly-coloured bird

BV (rains)

PLUMAGE Dark bluish-black mantle; pale chestnut-brown from forehead to nape; small deep-blue and white patches behind ear-coverts; **lilac-purple band from lower back to uppertail-coverts; white throat; tawny-yellow below;** crimson beak, legs. **Juv:** Yellowish beak.

HABITS Usually heard as it darts along forest streams, clearings; solitary or pairs; nests in mud walls; also catches insects. **Call: Distinctive high-pitched** *schi-scheee* squeal, somewhat subdued; usually in low flight or in vicinity of nest.

SGNP
KBS
Phansad
Tansa
Shyd
Matheran
occ suburban
Mumbai
Fairly common

INDIAN GREY HORNBILL *Ocyceros birostris*

20-22"

Noisy, long-tailed bird with diagnostic beak

R

All sites also occ Talzan, Manori, Gorai
Fairly common

PLUMAGE Pale brownish-grey; paler abdomen; darker cheeks, ear-coverts; in flight, whitish trailing-edge to wings; **long, graduated tail, tipped white; diagnostic curved, blackish beak, small pointed casque** (smaller in female).

HABITS Essentially arboreal; noisy and demonstrative; pairs, small bands (23 once sighted in SGNP); occ descends into bush; visits fruiting trees. **Call: Diagnostic loud, whistling squeals,** slightly melancholic in tone; calls on perch and in flight.

MALABAR PIED HORNBILL *A coronatus*

27"

Large black and white bird with huge beak

R

Phansad
Shyd
SGNP
Scarce

One or two pairs sighted SGNP since Feb 2000

PLUMAGE Black overall; in flight, **diagnostic white outertail feathers; trailing-edge to wings. Large, pale-yellow beak, with striking, black and yellow casque.** Orbital-patch pale-blue (male), pale-pinkish (female).

HABITS Arboreal; prefers tall forest; solitary or pairs; seen with other birds on fruiting trees. Call: Assortment of high-pitched, loud screams and chuckles.

BROWN-HEADED BARBET *Megalaima zeylanica*

11"

Highly vocal, green and brown bird

R

♪

PLUMAGE Brown head, neck, breast, finely-streaked whitish; rest of plumage grass-green; naked, pale-orange patch around eyes; swollen, dull pinkish-orange beak.

Most sites also occ Aarey
Fairly common

HABITS Arboreal; solitary or pairs; often difficult to sight; visits fruiting, flowering trees.
Call: Diagnostic, loud, ringing *kutroo* or *pukrook*; often begins with long-drawn *krrrrr*.

RELATED WHITE-CHEEKED BARBET *M viridis*
Pale-white cheeks, narrow supercilium; restricted to Shyd. Uncommon.

EURASIAN WRYNECK *Jynx torquilla*

6"

Dull-plumaged, sparrow-like bird of open forest and scrub

WV

 ♪

PLUMAGE Pale grey-brown and buff above, vermiculated (plumage appears nightjar-like); dark crown-stripe, eye-stripe; barred tail; pale-buff below, closely-marked darker, barred on throat, breast; streaked below.

SGNP
Phansad
Murbad
occ S Mumbai
also occ Talzan
Uncommon

HABITS Solitary or pairs; often overlooked; tail raised, hops on ground to feed on insects; clings to tree stems, branches; perches like passerines, crosswise. **Call:** Occ a nasal, shrill *chyeu* and a sharp *tch-ch*, several times in succession.

RUFOUS WOODPECKER *Celeus brachyurus*

10"

Chestnut-brown woodpecker of deciduous forest

R

♪

Most sites
Fairly common

PLUMAGE Chestnut-brown overall, duller about head; finely-barred black above, chiefly on wings, tail; **crimson patch around eye** (usually absent in female). Plumage varies from bright chestnut-brown to dull rufous-brown.

HABITS Typically around ball-shaped nests of Crematogaster tree ants; also on tree stems, branches; solitary or pairs; occ sucks sap from base of banana leaves (Suriamal); seen in mixed bird parties. **Call: Diagnostic, high-pitched, loud**, *kee-kee* or *kae* 3-4 times, like Common Myna; most vocal Feb-May (brdg).

STREAK-THROATED WOODPECKER *Picus xanthopygaeus*

12"

Greenish woodpecker with scaly underbody; Sexes differ

R

Mblswr
occ Phansad
Uncommon

PLUMAGE Olivish-green above, yellower lower-back; **crimson crown; white malar stripe; supercilium**; whitish spots on flight-feathers; buff below, **stippled with dark scaly markings. Female: Black crown.**

HABITS Jerkily moves along tree stems, branches; often descends to ground, picking ants, termites; pairs usually close by. **Call:** Not very vocal; occ faint *pick* call; drums Jan-Apr (brdg).

BLACK-RUMPED FLAMEBACK *Dinopium benghalense*

11"

Woodpecker with brilliant golden-yellow back. Sexes differ

R

PLUMAGE Brilliant golden-yellow back; **crimson crown, crest; black hind-neck,** rump, tail; white sides of head, neck, lightly marked black; **blackish flight-feathers, marked white;** scaly, black and white below. **Female:** Black fore-crown, stippled white.

Most sites also occ Aarey, Gorai
Fairly common

Nos dropped since early-1990s

HABITS Solitary or pairs; occ in mixed bird parties; mostly on stems, branches; seldom descends to ground. **Call:** Distinctive; **high-pitched scream;** calls both on perch and in flight; drums intermittently, more often Jan-Mar (brdg).

WHITE-NAPED WOODPECKER *Chrysocolaptes festivus*

12"

Conspicuous, golden-backed woodpecker with white on upper back

R

PLUMAGE Golden-olive mostly on wings; **crimson crest;** black scapulars joined to broad, black band from eye, down face-sides; **diagnostic broad, white 'V' on nape, hind-neck;** blackish wing-tips, tail; **distinctive black linear stripes on cheeks, throat. Female:** Yellowish crown.

Phansad
SGNP
Tansa
KBS
Tungar (lower)
Shyd
Uncommon

Nos declined since early-1990s

HABITS More wary than Black-rumped; usually pairs close by. **Call:** High-pitched scream, similar to Black-rumped's.

YELLOW-CROWNED WOODPECKER   *Dendrocopos mahrattensis*

7"

Small, black
and white
woodpecker

R

Most sites
Uncommon

*Nos fallen
considerably since
early-1990s*

PLUMAGE Pied; deep sooty-brown above, boldly marked white, incl wings, tail; **yellow-brown crown; scarlet on hind-crown**; brown neck-sides; streaked breast; pale-buff below; **diagnostic scarlet on abdomen. Female:** Lacks scarlet hind-crown.

HABITS Prefers open forest, groves; usually pairs close by; rather unobtrusive; often in mixed parties of small birds. **Call:** Distinctive, weak but sharp *klik* or *klick-rrrr*; drums Feb-May.

HEART-SPOTTED WOODPECKER   *Hemicircus canente*

6-7"

Small, chubby,
black and whitish,
crested bird

R

KBS
SGNP
Tungar
Phansad
Sajanpada
Jawahar
Tansa
Shyd
Uncommon

PLUMAGE Black above, incl crown, **noticeable crest**; large, **whitish wing-patch with blackish, heart-shaped markings**; pale-white throat; sooty-brown below; blackish tail; **in flight**, large white wing-patches. **Female: White forehead, fore-crown.**

HABITS Arboreal; active, quite busy-looking; usually pairs or small family bands; often in mixed parties. **Call:** Somewhat squeaky *clhik-clhick* interspersed with harsh *churrr*; also a pleasing, trilling *chwee-chwie* of 7-8 notes; drums Feb-Apr; often calls in flight.

BLACK-HOODED ORIOLE *Oriolus xanthornus*

10"

Bright yellow bird
with black head

R

PLUMAGE Bright golden-yellow overall; **jet-black head, throat, upper-breast;** extensive black in wings, tail; pinkish-red beak. **Juv:** Black-streaked chin, throat.

All sites
Fairly common

HABITS Strictly arboreal; usually pairs; active, often with other birds on flowering trees.
Call: **Rich, melodious, 3-noted fluty** *chou-yoyoi*, quite similar in tone to Treepie's; occ 1-2 notes; also harsh, grating alarm-notes.

RUFOUS TREEPIE *Dendrocitta vagabunda*

19"

Long-tailed,
rufous, grey
and white,
arboreal bird

R

PLUMAGE **Sooty-grey head,** neck, breast; **rich-rufous mantle;** extensive **pale-grey and black in wings and long, graduated tail** (at rest and in flight); buff-rufous below breast. **Juv:** Choco-brown head.

Most sites
Fairly common

HABITS Arboreal; occ forest-edge; pairs usually close by; occ descends into bush; often in mixed parties; short, dipping flight, a few noisy wing-beats followed by a glide. **Call:** 3-noted, fluty *ko-ke-li* or *bob-o-link* quite like Black-hooded Oriole's; **distinctive mix of raucous shrieks and melodious calls;** also a grating *khae-khae-khe* call.

ASHY DRONGO   *Dicrurus leucophaeus*

11-12"

Greyish bird with
long, forked tail

WV

♪

All sites
also occ Gorai,
Esselworld
Fairly common

*Good nos along
SGNP's Tulsi Rd*

PLUMAGE Distinctly slaty-grey above with very
little gloss (can appear paler-grey); deep-grey
below; long, **deeply-forked tail**; in good light,
crimson-orange eyes. Somewhat more slender
than Black Drongo.

HABITS Arboreal, chiefly tall forest, forest-edge;
usually several around; active and territorial,
especially on flowering trees (Red Silk Cotton,
Indian Coral), **insistently driving away intruding
birds**; often hawks winged insects. Call: Loud
2-3-noted whistle; quite vocal; mix of snappish
and musical call-notes.

WHITE-BELLIED DRONGO   *Dicrurus caerulescens*

10"

Small, blackish
Drongo with
white belly

R

SGNP
Tansa
Phansad
KBS
Tungar
Kohoj
Jawahar
Murbad
also occ Aarey
Uncommon

**PLUMAGE Indigo-black above, with slight
gloss**; deep-grey or slaty chin, throat, upper-
breast, fading into **diagnostic white lower-
breast, abdomen**; long, deep-forked tail (shorter
than Black's or Ashy's).

HABITS Largely arboreal; occ descends into
lower storey of tree for insects; pairs usually close
by; sometimes in mixed parties; occ forest-edges.
Call: Assortment of whistling call-notes; mix of
pleasantly-musical notes and harsh screams.

SPANGLED DRONGO *Dicrurus hottentottus*

13"

Heavy-looking, iridescent, black bird with distinctive tail

R/LM

PLUMAGE Jet-black, with glossy, metallic sheen (can appear blue-black); **diagnostic long tail, outer feathers conspicuously upturned at tip; tuft of long, hair-like feathers over crown.**

HABITS Arboreal; solitary or pairs; often on flowering Indian Coral, Red Silk Cotton trees. Call: Very vocal; noisy and querulous, harsh screams and cheery whistling calls; good mimic.

RELATED BRONZED DRONGO *D aeneus* 9" **WV** Highly glossy; slight fork in longish tail; sighted SGNP, KBS, Tansa, Phansad. Uncommon.

SGNP
KBS
Phansad
Tungar
Murbad
Shyd
Elephanta
Matheran
Uncommon

GREATER RACKET-TAILED DRONGO *Dicrurus paradiseus*

13" + c. 12" tail

Noisy, glossy-black bird with distinctive tail

R

PLUMAGE Black, with metallic-bluish sheen; crest of plume-like feathers over forehead; **diagnostic tail**, slightly forked, with **highly-elongated, wiry outer feathers, ending in twisted 'rackets'.** Young birds and some adults lack tail-streamers.

HABITS Arboreal but frequently descends into bush to hawk insects; pairs or small bands; often in mixed bird parties; seen attacking Serpent Eagle, Shikra. Call: **Highly vocal, querulous**; assortment of screams, whistles; excellent mimic, imitating several birds (at least 19 species recorded); may call well before dawn.

SGNP
KBS
Tansa
Phansad
Murbad
Sajanpada
occ Mblswr
Fairly common

COMMON IORA *Aegithina tiphia*

5"

Arboreal, largely black and yellow bird. Sexes differ

R

♪ ● ●

All sites
occ S Mumbai
also occ
Esselworld
Fairly common

PLUMAGE Brdg Male: **Black above** (occ suffused with slight yellow); **greenish-yellow rump; white bars** across dark wings; black tail; **yellow below.** Non-brdg Male: Olive-green above; yellower forehead. Female: **Yellow-green above;** pale-yellow below.

HABITS Largely arboreal; pairs often close by; probes foliage for insects, spiders; often in mixed parties; also urban parks, tree-dotted cultivation. Call: **Diagnostic 2-noted whistling** *wheeeee-tchu*, second syllable very short; brdg male (May-Aug) has short trilling song; occ harsh alarm-notes.

COMMON WOODSHRIKE *Tephrodornis pondicerianus*

7"

Pale grey-brown bird of light forest and scrub

R

♪ ●

Most sites
also Gorai,
Esselworld
Fairly common

PLUMAGE Ashy-brown above; broad **whitish stripe over eye, bordered by dark band below** (through eyes); dark-brown **tail with white outer feathers;** paler ashy-brown below, whiter on chin, throat.

HABITS Prefers open forest, forest-edge, tree-dotted cultivation; keeps to lower and middle storey; unobtrusive; pairs usually close by, occ descending into bush; active and vocal when brdg (Mar-May). Call: Pleasant, whistling *wheet-wheet* often followed by quick-repeated *whi-whi-whi-whi*; short, trilling song when brdg.

BLACK-HEADED CUCKOOSHRIKE *Coracina melanoptera*

8"

Black-headed, greyish, arboreal bird. Sexes differ

R

♪

PLUMAGE Jet-black head, neck, upper-breast; dark-grey mantle, rump; **blackish wings, tail**, with some grey and whitish; dull ashy-grey below breast, fading into white below. Female: **Lacks black head; whitish below, barred darker.**

HABITS Largely arboreal; **active and inquisitive**; pairs usually together, may associate in mixed bird parties. Call: Whistling song of several notes (May-Aug); higher-pitched first note.

SGNP
Phansad
KBS
Tungar
Shyd
Matheran
also occ Aarey,
Gorai
Uncommon

LARGE CUCKOOSHRIKE *Coracina macei*

12"

Stocky, pale-coloured, forest bird. Sexes differ

R

♪

PLUMAGE Pale-grey above; black on face-sides (dark band through eyes); pale-grey throat, upper-breast, fading into **white below; white tail-tips.** Female: Whitish below, barred grey.

HABITS Strictly arboreal; occ forest-edge; often solitary; seldom few together; moves much from tree to tree; **strong, slightly-dipping flight.** Call: **Diagnostic**, often revealing bird's presence in area; calls chiefly in flight over forest; loud 2-noted *tchi-eee* or *tchie-yee*, with distinctly inquisitive tone, like Plum-headed Parakeet's.

SGNP
Tansa
Phansad
KBS
Shyd
Sajanpada
Uncommon

SCARLET MINIVET *Pericrocotus flammeus*

8-9"

Arboreal, black
and scarlet
(male) or yellow
(female) bird

R

SGNP
KBS
Phansad
Shyd
Matheran
Elephanta
Uncommon

**PLUMAGE Jet-black head, back, wings; broad
scarlet wing-band** and smaller scarlet spot (on
secondaries); **scarlet rump; black and scarlet tail;
scarlet below throat. Female:** Greyish above;
yellow forehead, rump; yellow in wings and tail;
yellow below.

HABITS Strictly arboreal; usually pairs; small
bands in winter (11 birds Yeur Hills once);
occ in mixed parties; sallies after winged insects.
Call: Distinctive 2-noted *whee-chwee* or *where-chichie* whistle.

SMALL MINIVET *Pericrocotus cinnamomeus*

6"

Slender,
long-tailed,
arboreal bird.
Sexes differ

R

Most sites
also occ Gorai,
Aarey
Uncommon

PLUMAGE Sooty-grey above; pale-scarlet patch
on wings; scarlet outertail feathers; **jet-black
chin, throat, face-sides;** scarlet-orange and
yellowish below. **Female:** Dull-grey above;
yellow-orange rump; dingy-white below,
suffused with dull orange-yellow.

HABITS Arboreal; occ orchards, tree-dotted
cultivation; active; pairs or small bands; **short
sallies after winged insects;** sometimes hovers;
seen in mixed bird parties. Call: Soft, cheerful
tsfee-tsvee.

GOLDEN-FRONTED LEAFBIRD *Chloropsis aurifrons*

8"

Bright-green, richly-voiced, arboreal bird

R

PLUMAGE Bright-green overall; **diagnostic golden-orange forehead; blackish chin, throat,** bordered by purplish-blue moustachial bands; faint yellow border around throat. Juv: Light-green chin, throat.

HABITS Strictly arboreal; usually pairs close by; **very vocal but difficult to locate;** active and somewhat belligerent, especially when in mixed bird parties on flowering trees. Call: Loud *che-chwit*, quite like Black Drongo's or Shikra's; rich range of whistling notes; excellent mimic.

SGNP
KBS
Phansad
Tungar
Tansa
Jawahar
Sajanpada
Shyd
Fairly common

BLUE-WINGED LEAFBIRD *Chloropsis cochinchinensis*

8"

Grass-green bird with blue in wings

R

PLUMAGE Bright-green overall; **greenish-yellow forehead; purplish-blue moustachial stripe; less extensive black on chin, throat, but brighter yellow border around face, throat;** small, bright-blue patch on wings. Female: **Blue-green chin, throat.**

HABITS Like Golden-fronted; often with other birds; prefers light forest, forest-edge. Call: Rich voiced, with wide range of whistles; **excellent mimic.**

SGNP
Shyd
Sajanpada
Jawahar
Tansa
also occ Aarey
Uncommon

RED-WHISKERED BULBUL *Pycnonotus jocosus*

8"

Lively, dark-brown and white, crested bird

R

All sites
Common

PLUMAGE Distinctive head-pattern; **black head, upright crest; white cheek, red patch below eye (whiskers)**; white tips to outertail feathers; **white below, with incomplete, dark gorget; bright-red vent.** Juv: Lacks red whiskers.

HABITS Usually pairs or small, roving bands; active and cheery, quite confiding at hill-stations; present in every mixed bird party, occ even in urban parks, groves. **Call: Distinctive 3-4 noted, lively, whistling notes;** harsh alarm-notes.

WHITE-BROWED BULBUL *Pycnonotus luteolus*

8"

A pale-olivish bird of thick bush growth

R

Most sites
occ creeksides
Fairly common

PLUMAGE Pale olive-brown above, somewhat brighter on wings; prominent **white supercilium, small streak below eyes**; yellowish rump; dingy-white below (may have slight yellow wash); **brighter yellow undertail.**

HABITS Usually difficult to sight bird of dense shrubbery; periodically appears on bush-top, overhead wires or dashes across path or clearing; pairs or up to 4-5 birds around; calls indicative of presence in area. **Call: Diagnostic bubbling, whistling chatter,** loud and sudden; various notes seem to fall over one another.

BLACK BULBUL *Hypsipetes leucocephalus*

9"

Arboreal, dark-grey bird of hill-forests

R

Shyd
occ Matheran
Uncommon

PLUMAGE Dark slaty-grey overall (can appear almost blackish); **black forehead, short scruffy crest**; long tail very slightly forked; **diagnostic coral-red beak, legs.**

HABITS A bird of hill-forests; strictly arboreal, keeping to leafy canopy; usually small, wandering bands; often with other birds in mixed parties; makes short sallies after winged insects.
Call: Distinctive shrill whistling calls; 2-noted *wheu-wee* occ preceded by a loud *shwekee*; also harsh alarm-notes.

YELLOW-BROWED BULBUL *Iole indica*

8"

Noisy, bright-olivish and yellow bird of hill-forest

R

Bhmshnkr
Mblswr
Uncommon

PLUMAGE Olive above, with yellowish wash; yellower face-sides, **supercilium; brighter yellow below.** Blackish beak.

HABITS Keeps to hill-forest; usually several around with other small birds in mixed parties; restless and noisy; spends much time in undergrowth; also ascends into canopy; regularly on flowering, fruiting trees. **Call:** Distinctive; **soft but melodious whistling notes**; common call a 2-3-noted *whiech-whee* and *chi-whi-tchup*; also harsh alarm-notes.

PUFF-THROATED BABBLER   *Pellorneum ruficeps*

6"

Skulking, olive-brown bird with diagnostic call

R

♪

Most sites
Fairly common

PLUMAGE Olivish-brown above, with **dark-rufous crown; pale-buff supercilium;** whitish throat merges into dull buff-white below; **boldly-streaked breast, flanks.**

HABITS Keeps to forest undergrowth; frequently clambers up to middle storey; usually pairs; hops and rummages on forest floor; momentarily emerges in open or flits across clearing.
Call: Diagnostic, rich 3-4-noted whistle, best interpreted as *pee-tee-swee* or '*he-will-beat-you*'; lengthy song (late-Apr-Aug), of up to 20-28 syllables, rambling in scale; occ harsh alarm-notes.

BROWN-CHEEKED FULVETTA   *Alcippe poioicephala*

6"

Dull-brownish, forest-bird with greyish head

R

♪

Shyd (Mblswr, Bhmshnkr)
SGNP
Tungar
Matheran
Phansad
KBS
Fairly common

PLUMAGE Ashy-grey crown, nape, merges into more **olive-brown mantle;** rufous-brown wings, tail; pale-buff below, darker breast, flanks.

HABITS Active and vocal; moves much between undergrowth and middle storey, occ emerging in clearings; usually several around; often in mixed bird parties. **Call: Diagnostic 5-6-noted, musical whistle,** best interpreted as '*daddy-give-me-choc-late*'; also harsh alarm-notes.

INDIAN SCIMITAR BABBLER *Pomatorhinus horsfieldii*

9"

Earthy-brown and white bird with long, curved beak

R

♪

SGNP
Phansad
Tansa
Tungar
KBS
Shyd
Uncommon

PLUMAGE Dark earthy-brown above; striking, **white supercilium** extends to hind-neck; **broad black band through eye**, continuing down sides of neck and breast; white below; **diagnostic, long, gently-curving, yellowish beak**.

HABITS Skulker, often heard, rarely clearly seen; rummages on ground or clambers around middle storey; usually pairs; sometimes in mixed bird parties. Call: Diagnostic fluty 3-4-noted *whou-tu-tu-tu* whistle, with hardly any pause between notes; also a short, rolling, *pkrrukru* bubbling call, sometimes as an add-on.

JUNGLE BABBLER *Turdoides striatus*

10"

Untidy-looking, long-tailed, brownish bird

R

 ♪

All sites
also occ Gorai,
Vikhroli, Aarey,
Navi Mumbai
Fairly common

PLUMAGE Dull earthy-brown above, faintly-streaked; dark wings; **diagnostic rufous rump, long, graduated tail**; dull tawny-grey below, with pale and dark tints to feathers; **pale-yellow eyes, beak, legs**.

HABITS Noisy, gregarious, and inquisitive; small bands of 5-8 birds; rummages on ground; also visits flowering, fruiting trees; often in mixed bird parties. Call: **Diagnostic chattering notes**; intermittently bursts into **loud, discordant, almost hysterical babble** at slightest sign of intrusion.

TAWNY-BELLIED BABBLER *Dumetia hyperythra*

5"

Small, olive-
brown bird of
undergrowth

R

Most sites
also occ Aarey,
Gorai,
Esselworld
Fairly common

PLUMAGE Olive-brown above, with slight rufous
wash; **dull reddish-brown fore-crown**; longish
tail, graduated, faintly cross-rayed (seen in good
light); **diagnostic white throat; fulvous sides of
face, underbody.**

Sighted Malabar
Hill late-1980s

HABITS Inveterate skulker in undergrowth;
occ clambers into canopy; usually several around,
by themselves or in mixed bird parties; sometimes
emerges into open but soon dives into cover.
Call: Feeble *sweesh* or *sweeece*; some soft but
grating, cheeping calls; several may call together
when agitated.

BLACK-NAPED MONARCH *Hypothymis azurea*

6"

Active,
bluish bird of
deciduous forest

R

♪

All sites
also occ Alibaug,
Gorai
Fairly common

PLUMAGE **Bright sky-blue** overall, fading into
whitish below breast; **diagnostic jet-black patch
on nape, narrow gorget on upper-breast.**
Female: Duller overall; **lacks black nape-patch,
breast-gorget.**

HABITS Active and fidgety; pairs usually close
by; flits about, often in mixed parties of small
insectivorous birds; commoner in deciduous
forest. Call: **Distinctive, somewhat high-pitched**
chae-chweich, similar to Paradise-flycatcher's but
softer; a loud *chwae-chuwe-chuwee* (brdg Apr-Sep),
like Tailorbird's but more rapid.

RED-THROATED FLYCATCHER *Ficedula parva*

5"

Small, brown bird with white in tail

WV

PLUMAGE Brown above; **ashy head**; dark tail has **diagnostic white patches at base of outer feathers** (best seen when flicked or in flight); **orangish-rufous throat, upper-breast** (variable in richness). **Female:** **Dull-white throat;** buff-white breast.

Most sites occ S Mumbai, also occ Gorai, Aarey
Fairly common

HABITS Prefers shaded areas, rarely high in foliage; often descends to ground; solitary; active, alert; flicks tail often; occ urban parks, groves. **Call:** Distinctive, jarring *dttrrr*-like sound made by rubbing tongue on roof of mouth; occ a *klik-klikrrr* or a somber *pfee* alarm-note.

GREY-HEADED CANARY FLYCATCHER *Culicicapa ceylonensis*

5"

Lively, grey, yellow and greenish bird

WV

PLUMAGE Diagnostic **ashy-grey head, neck, throat and upper-breast;** yellowish-green above; **yellowish below breast**.

SGNP
Kohoj
Phansad
KBS
Shyd
Elephanta
Uncommon

HABITS Mostly tall forest; normally solitary; also amid mixed parties of small birds; **active and restless**. **Call:** Calls regularly; fairly loud and distinctive trilling call; occ a soft *tchichrrr* during short sallies.

Sighted late-May near Mblswr

VERDITER FLYCATCHER *Eumyias thalassina*

6"

Active, verditer-blue bird of forest

WV

KBS
Phansad
SGNP
Shyd
Jawahar
Khopoli
Uncommon

PLUMAGE Bright verditer-blue overall; **distinctive black lores.** Female: Duller overall, appearing grey-blue (difference most apparent when both sexes together).

HABITS Prefers open forest, edges; pairs usually close by; perches quite erect; restless; makes frequent short sallies; often with other small insectivorous birds; sometimes mistaken for Black-naped Monarch. Call: Occ calls in winter; a soft *tzwee*, possibly an alarm-note (heard KBS).

TICKELL'S BLUE FLYCATCHER *Cyornis tickelliae*

6"

Dark-blue bird with orangish throat

R

Most sites occ S&C,
suburban Mumbai
also occ Powai,
Vikhroli, Malvani,
Gorai, Aarey
Fairly common

PLUMAGE Male: **Dark indigo-blue above,** darker on lores; indistinct, paler supercilium; **rusty-orange throat, breast,** quite clearly cut-off from white below. Female: Duller overall; paler, less extensive orange on throat, breast.

HABITS Prefers shaded areas, in forest and grove; usually pairs in vicinity; often with other small birds. Call: **Diagnostic; calls often; fluty, whistling trill** of 5-9 notes, occ preceded by *tlick* or *tick-tik* note; sometimes snatches of this trill in alarm; sings more frequently Apr-Aug.

ASIAN PARADISE-FLYCATCHER *Terpsiphone paradisi*

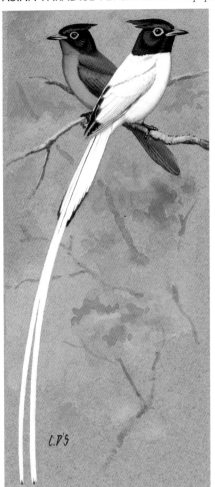

Male 8"+ c.10" tail
Female 8"

Long-tailed, black
and white or
chestnut bird.
Sexes differ

WV

● ● ♪

All sites
occ S&C,
suburban Mumbai
Fairly common

*Brdg record Gorai
(1970s), reportedly
Lonavala (1990)*

PLUMAGE Long tail-sreamers, 10-12"; **silvery-white overall**,
faintly streaked black on back; **glossy blue-black head, crest**;
black in wings. **RUFOUS PHASE**: Rufous-chestnut overall.
Female and Juv Male: **Lack tail-streamers**; rufous-chestnut above;
ashy-grey chin, throat, upper-breast, fading to dull ashy-white.

HABITS Keeps to shaded areas; often solitary; occ pairs close
by; arboreal but may descend into bush; frequently sallies, darts
across clearings; often in urban parks, groves. **Call**: Diagnostic,
fairly harsh *chwae* or *chchwae*; soft, warbling song of brdg male
(once SGNP mid-Jun).

WHITE-RUMPED SHAMA *Copsychus malabaricus*

10"

Long-tailed, black
and chestnut
forest bird.
Sexes differ

R

♪

KBS
Phansad
Tungar
SGNP
Shyd
Matheran
Murbad
Fairly common

PLUMAGE Lustrous-black above (slight bluish gloss); **white rump** and much of **outertail feathers**; black throat, upper-breast; orange-chestnut below. **Female: Slaty-brown** where male is black; rufous below, paler on abdomen. Juv: Browner, speckled.

HABITS Prefers shaded forest; seen along clearings, jungle paths; occ feeds on ground; wary, sometimes hunts flycatcher-like.
Call: **Diagnostic; rich musical whistles**; most vocal May-Aug (brdg); intermittently other times; also various grating calls, incl alarm-notes.

MALABAR WHISTLING THRUSH *Myophonus horsfieldii*

10"

Blue-black bird of
forest streams

R

♪

Shyd
Matheran
SGNP
KBS
Phansad
Jawahar
Fairly common

*Nests found SGNP,
KBS, Mblswr,
Malshej*

PLUMAGE Deep, glistening, blue-black overall, more vivid-blue on wings, tail; bright, **cobalt-blue on forehead, shoulder-patch.**
Juv: Sooty-brown with bluish on wings, tail.

HABITS Usually along rocky forest streams, waterfalls (rains); active and wary; solitary or pairs; settles on roadside culverts in hill areas, invariably 'diving' into a drop upon approach.
Call: **Diagnostic, famed 'whistling-schoolboy'** melodious rambling whistle of amazingly human quality; most vocal May-Aug (brdg); also a high-pitched screech in low flight.

ORANGE-HEADED THRUSH *Zoothera citrina*

9"

Blue-grey and orange-chestnut bird

R

PLUMAGE Rufous-orange head, neck; bluish-grey wash to wings, tail; white patch on wing-shoulder; **diagnostic white face-sides** with 2 short, dark-brown stripes; white chin, throat; rufous-orange below. Female: **More olive-brown** than blue-grey.

HABITS Shade-loving, rather shy bird; pairs usually close by; rummages amid leaf-litter on damp ground. Call: Distinctive; whistling song (May-Aug), rambling in scale, generally weak in tone; also a harsh screech.

SGNP
KBS
Phansad
Shyd
Matheran
Tungar
Tansa
also occ Aarey
Fairly common

BLUE-CAPPED ROCK THRUSH *Monticola cinclorhynchus*

7-8"

Blue and chestnut-orange forest bird. Sexes differ

WV

PLUMAGE Cobalt-blue head, chin, throat; broad black stripe through eyes, extending to dark mantle, wings; conspicuous **white wing-patch;** chestnut-orange rump, breast, underbody. Female: **Olive-brown above;** dull-buff below, scaled/speckled dark-brown.

HABITS Largely shaded forest; normally solitary; rummages amid leaf-litter or keeps to lower storey, occ making short sallies after insects; generally silent, shy and wary; often overlooked.

SGNP
KBS
Tungar
Phansad
Shyd
Tansa
Sajanpada
Kohoj
Uncommon

EURASIAN BLACKBIRD *Turdus merula*

10"

Deep-grey bird
with black cap.
Sexes differ

R/LM

♪

Shyd (breeds)
occ KBS,
Phansad, SGNP
Uncommon

PLUMAGE Slaty-grey overall; **blackish cap,**
wings, tail. **Orange-yellow beak, legs.**
Female: Dark ashy-brown above; paler below,
speckled/streaked darker.

HABITS Prefers shaded areas; pairs or several in
an area; hops and rummages on ground; often
settles in trees; occ in mixed bird parties.
Call: Distinctive; **melodious whistling song**
(brdg male, Apr-Jul); occ interspersed with
imitations of other bird-calls; also various grating
call-notes, snatches of song during other months.

FOREST WAGTAIL *Dendronanthus indicus*

7"

Olive-brown bird
with conspicuous
wing and breast
markings

WV

SGNP
KBS
Phansad
Sajanpada
Shyd
also occ Gorai
Uncommon

PLUMAGE Dull olive-brown above; whitish
supercilium; **dark wings with conspicuous pale
yellow-white bands;** whitish outertail feathers;
pale-white below; **diagnostic 2 broad, black
gorgets.**

HABITS Forest clearings, wide trails; often
solitary; **diagnostic, sideways (not up and
down) movement of tail;** wary, taking to tree
branches upon slightest alarm. **Call:** Quick, sharp
tziff, usually when flying into trees.

PALE-BILLED FLOWERPECKER *Dicaeum erythrorynchos*

3-4"

Restless, arboreal, dull-coloured bird

R

PLUMAGE Dull olive-brown above, with faint ashy wash; browner wings; dark-brown tail; **pale ashy-white below**; at close range, **diagnostic pale (flesh-pink) beak**.

HABITS Open forest, groves; strictly arboreal, highly active; solitary or pairs, invariably attending to epiphytic plants (Loranthus, Viscum) on large trees; swallows fruit whole. **Call:** Fairly loud and vocal; sharp *chik-chik* akin to sound produced by rubbing tongue on roof of mouth; occ mixed with sharp twitter; also short twittering song when brdg (Mar-Jul).

Most sites also occ Gorai, Esselworld
Fairly common

THICK-BILLED FLOWERPECKER *Dicaeum agile*

4"

Tiny, dull-coloured bird of forest

R

PLUMAGE Ashy-brown above, with dull-olive wash; pale olive-green rump; dark tail (narrowly tipped white); **faintly streaked on breast, flanks** (at close range); slaty-grey beak.

HABITS Largely arboreal; occ descends into bush; plucks fruit, doesn't swallow whole; often jerks tail. **Call:** Similar to but shriller than Pale-billed.

RELATED PLAIN FLOWERPECKER *D concolor* Darker olive-brown above; **blackish beak**; pale buff-white below; observed Phansad, KBS, Mblswr, Bhmshnkr. Uncommon.

SGNP
Phansad
KBS
Tungar
Jawahar
Shyd
Uncommon

PURPLE SUNBIRD *Nectarinia asiatica*

4"

Tiny, dazzling, restless bird. Sexes differ

R

♪ ● ●

All sites
S&C, suburban
Mumbai
Common

PLUMAGE Male (brdg): **Iridescent purplish-blue** sheen overall; **orange-scarlet pectoral tufts**; narrow, coppery-chestnut breast-band. Female: Olivish-brown above; **pale supercilium** (sometimes indistinct); **uniform pale-yellow below**. Non-brdg Male: Like female but diagnostic purple-black stripe down centre of throat to belly.

HABITS **Restless bird** of foliage; invariably around flowering plants. Call: Distinctive *chweet-chweet*, livelier than Purple-rumped's; brdg male (Mar-Jul, occ Oct-Nov) has loud, animated song.

LOTEN'S SUNBIRD *Nectarinia lotenia*

5"

Purplish-blue bird with long, curved beak. Sexes differ

R

♪

SGNP
KBS
Phansad
Tungar
Shyd (foothills)
also occ Alibaug,
Murud
Fairly common

PLUMAGE Blackish above, with iridescent blue-green sheen; small yellow tufts on breast-sides; deep sooty-brown below with **diagnostic maroon band across breast**; long, sharply-curved beak. Female: Dark olive-brown above, dull-yellow below.

HABITS More arboreal than other sunbirds; pairs or solitary; often at edge of forest. Call: Rather vocal; tone similar to Purple's.

CRIMSON SUNBIRD *Aethopyga siparaja*

Male 6"
Female 4"

Long-tailed sunbird with scarlet throat and breast. Sexes differ

R

PLUMAGE Dull-crimson mantle; **metallic-green crown, long tail**; bright-yellow rump (not easily seen); **bright-scarlet chin, throat, breast.** Female: Dull olive-green above; pale olive-yellow below. In eclipse plumage may have very pale-crimson throat, breast.

HABITS Chiefly forest, forest-edges; active and restless between canopy and bush; pairs often close by. Call: Sharp *tzip* or *tzsip*, fairly loud and animated in tone; brdg male (Jun-Sep) has trilling song.

SGNP
KBS
Phansad
Tungar
Shyd
Uncommon

CRIMSON-BACKED SUNBIRD *Nectarinia minima*

4"

Tiny, restless, iridescent bird. Sexes differ

R

PLUMAGE Overall quite like Purple-rumped; **more crimson mantle, scapulars**, with slight maroon wash; **diagnostic crimson breast-band**; pale-yellow below. Female: More olivish above; pale-yellow below, duller on throat; crimson-brown rump. Smaller size, finer beak.

HABITS **Active and restive**; pairs or even several around, usually on and around flowering plants; possibly in mixed bird parties. Call: Metallic *tchik-tchik*; squeaky song intermittently round the year but more often Oct-Apr.

Shyd
Phansad
occ KBS
Uncommon

ORIENTAL WHITE-EYE *Zosterops palpebrosus*

4"

Tiny, olive-yellow
bird with white
eye-ring

R/LM

Most sites
Uncommon

PLUMAGE Olive-yellow above, browner on
wings, tail; blackish lores; **diagnostic white eye-ring**; **bright-yellow chin, throat** and undertail
contrast with pale-white breast, belly.

HABITS Arboreal; keeps to middle and lower
storey; **active and sociable**, often several by
themselves or in mixed bird parties; sighted on
numerous flowering plants. **Call:** Faint *tseer*, often
when flying from tree to tree; also a somewhat
petulant *chae-chee*; short jingling song of brdg
male (Mar-Sep; heard Mblswr, Pnchgni, Phansad).

CHESTNUT-SHOULDERED PETRONIA *Petronia xanthocollis*

5-6"

Arboreal, dull-
coloured, forest-
dwelling sparrow

R/LM

All sites
Fairly common

**PLUMAGE Pale ashy-brown above; darker wings
with 2 white bars** and **chestnut shoulder-patch**
(over the broader, top white bar); dull ashy-white
below; in clear light, **diagnostic pale-yellow
throat-patch. Female:** Paler, **rufous-brown
shoulder-patch.**

HABITS Arboreal; pairs or small bands, often in
tall trees; flocks during winter (about 200 sighted
near Kanheri); often feeds on ground and visits
flowering trees. **Call:** Chirping call-notes often
reveal bird's presence; rather monotonous,
chirping notes, softer than House Sparrow's.

GREENISH WARBLER *Phylloscopus trochiloides*

4-5"

Active, dull-greenish bird of leafy branches

WV

PLUMAGE Dull-green above; in fresh plumage (Oct) **pale-yellowish wing-bar** (sometimes indistinct); conspicuous **buff supercilium**; dirty-white below, usually with faint yellow wash.

HABITS Chiefly arboreal; solitary or several around; occ in mixed bird parties.
Call: **Diagnostic cheery** *shwei-ees*; rapid, short, trilling song (Oct, late-Mar/early-Apr).

RELATED HUME'S *P humei* Grey-green above; pale-buff wing-bar, supercilium; occ a fairly clear *veest* call; SGNP, Gorai, Suriamal. Uncommon.

SGNP
KBS
Phansad
Tansa
Tungar
Elephanta
Matheran
Shyd
Jawahar
occ S&C,
suburban
Mumbai
Common

GREAT TIT *Parus major*

5"

Lively, grey, black and white bird

R/LM

PLUMAGE Jet-black head, throat, breast and abdomen centre; **conspicuous white cheeks**; ashy-grey above with faint-bluish tinge; whitish sides of underbody; black, ashy-grey and white tail.

HABITS Restless, inquisitive and noisy; often in mixed bird parties. Call: Distinctive, lively *whi-chi-chee* whistle; other bubbly notes (summer) and grating alarm-note.

occ Murbad
also occ Shahpur,
Tansa, LK,
Mblswr
Uncommon

GRASS & SCRUB

Open country: grass and scrublands, tree-dotted cultivation, edges of forests, creeks and marshes.

Aarey
Alibaug North (Alibaug-Mandwa-Saral)
Alibaug South (Alibaug-Murud-Agardanda)
Gorai (Manori to Uttan, incl Esselworld)
Kalyan (Shil Jn to Badlapur, MIDC Rd, base of Matheran Range)
Karjat (Chowk Jn to Kashele and Badlapur, Palasdhare to Hamrapur)
Khopoli (along Pali Rd, Pen Rd)
Malvani (incl AIR grounds, Marve Jn-Aksa-Madh)
Manor (along and west of NH-8, from Varai to Manor)
Mumbai (Bhavan's campus, Juhu airfield, Kalina, Racecourse)
Murbad (to base of Malshej Ghat, and south to Barvi)
Navi Mumbai (incl areas along Parsik Hills)
Panvel (Navi Mumbai to Panvel, base of Matheran Range, JNPT Rd)
Shahpur (along NH-8, from Bhiwandi Jn up to Shahpur Jn, incl
approach routes to Tansa and Vaitarna)
Shirsat (along NH-8 from Dahisar Check Naka to Varai)
Talzan (eastern side of Manori Creek)
Uran (along Palm Beach Rd to Funde-Panje-Uran)
Vadhkal (Vadhkal Jn to Alibaug and Poynad-Nagothane)
Vikhroli (chiefly areas in Godrej Pirojshanagar)
Wada (areas east of NH-8, from Varai Jn to Kasa)

BLACK-SHOULDERED KITE *Elanus caeruleus*

13"

Small, grey-white and black raptor

R/LM

PLUMAGE Pale-grey above; **black patch around red eyes; diagnostic black shoulder-patch, seen at rest and in flight; white below; in OH flight, pale body, black wing-tips.** Juv: Darker; dull grey-brown.

Most sites
Fairly common
(Sep-Mar)

Very few breed; nest found Kalyan

HABITS Solitary or several scattered in an area; perches regularly on overhead cables; leisurely flight, usually under 20 m; **hovers in mid-air**, scanning below for insects, rodents. Call: Occ weakish *kreee-ee* squeal (heard May, around nest).

PALLID HARRIER *Circus macrourus*

17-19"

Slender, pale greyish-white raptor of open country. Sexes differ

WV

PLUMAGE Pale-grey above; whitish below; **in flight, whitish body with black wing-tips.** Female: Brownish; **distinct head-pattern,** pale-buff stripes around eyes; narrow, whitish rump-patch (in flight); pale-buff below, streaked darker; **OH flight,** dark bands on pale flight-feathers.

Panvel
Uran
Vadhkal
Karjat
Shahpur
Murbad
Alibaug-N,S
Vikhroli
Uncommon

HABITS In plains and hill country; usually solitary; flies low over ground; graceful, sailing flight.

RELATED **HEN HARRIER** *C cyaneus* Deeper-grey above; more extensive black on wing-tips. Female: Broader white rump-patch. Uncommon.

SHORT-TOED SNAKE EAGLE *Circaetus gallicus*

25-27"

Heavy-looking, brown and white raptor

LM/WV

Shirsat
Khopoli-Karjat
Uran
Manor
Kalyan
Aarey
Navi Mumbai
Uncommon

PLUMAGE Variable ashy-brown above; **pale-buff or almost whitish below**; throat and upper-breast lightly streaked; in OH flight, pale body, underwings, faintly-banded; dark-banded tail, broadest near tail-tip; **wings held level in soaring flight**. Unfeathered tarsus.

HABITS Largely solitary; wanders much; circles high or glides low; occ hovers; **dives swiftly on prey**. Call: Loud, somewhat plaintive *peeaou*; heard Manor (Feb); calls mostly in flight.

BOOTED EAGLE *Hieraaetus pennatus*

21"

Small, long-tailed eagle

WV

Aarey
Wada
Manor
Karjat
Vadhkal
Navi Mumbai
Uncommon

PLUMAGE **Has dark and pale phases, pale commoner.** Buff-brown above, with **pale shoulder-patches**; in OH flight, **whitish below, with dark flight-feathers**; may show pale patch on inner-primaries; wings held level in soaring flight. **DARK PHASE**: Uniform deeper-brown above; paler tail.

HABITS Over open and forest-edge terrain; graceful flight; sometimes flies low over ground or over forest canopy, hawk-like through trees; pairs often close by; regularly soars. Call: Shrill *keeee* in flight, fading towards end.

WHITE-RUMPED VULTURE *Gyps bengalensis* 35"

PLUMAGE Dark-brown overall; naked, **grey-brown head, neck** with dingy-white ruff; **in OH flight, dark body and paler flight-feathers** contrast with whitish underwing-coverts; **diagnostic white lower-back, rump,** best visible in flight from above or when bird turns/banks in flight. Juv: Brownish, with whiter head, darker underwings; lacks white rump.

HABITS Gregarious; soars high, sometimes with other raptors, large waterbirds.

(1) Dark-brownish vulture with white on lower-back
R/LM

●

Khopoli-Karjat
Murbad
Manor
Wada
Shirsat
Aarey
Alibaug-N,S
Uncommon

LONG-BILLED VULTURE *Gyps indicus* 36-38"

PLUMAGE Pale sandy-brown overall, variably edged darker; **blackish head, neck; OH flight, pale below, with dark flight-feathers.** Juv: Darker above, with paler head.

HABITS Often with White-rumped; soars regularly.

RELATED EURASIAN GRIFFON *G fulvus* **LM** Slightly larger; pale-white head; dull rufous-brown below, streaked; in OH flight more rufous-brown underbody and pale band along median underwing-coverts; known to breed sporadically on rock-faces in Shyd. Uncommon.

(2) Sandy-brown, large vulture with pale underbody
R/LM

Khopoli-Karjat
Kalyan
Murbad
also Shyd
Uncommon

Few brdg sites with very small populations – nos fallen alarmingly since mid-1990s

AQUILAS EAGLES

Complex group of large raptors (25-34"), mostly seen Sep-Nov; sporadically up to Feb/early-Mar; generally brownish with yellowish legs, cere; field identification difficult. The Deonar and Gorai landfill sites and transmission towers along Vashi bridge on Thane Creek are excellent spots to view roosting eagles, kites, other raptors. All descriptions pertain to adult phase.

WV/LM

(1) **LESSER SPOTTED** *Aquila pomarina* In flight, may show **faint-white on uppertail-coverts**; in OH flight, pale leading-edge to wings; **whitish carpal-patches** (often double); lesser spray to wing-tips; usually over forest; sometimes around lakes, marshes.

(2) **GREATER SPOTTED** *A clanga* Darker-brown; may be lightly speckled; distinctly more thickset than Lesser; in flight, may show some white on uppertail-coverts; in OH flight, shorter, rounder tail, broader wings than Lesser; more splayed wing-tips; **usually dark leading-edge to wings**; often only one carpal-patch, occ indistinct; **when gliding, wings droop prominently at carpals**; flatter when soaring; usually around wetlands, marshes, occ over forest.

TAWNY EAGLE *A rapax* Varies from dark-brown to buff-brown; in flight **lacks white on uppertail-coverts**; may show small buff-yellow on nape; occ slight pale patch on inner-primaries; in OH flight, head, neck stick out more; darker underwings; can have paler form, creamy-buff above and below, with darker flight-feathers; open areas, landfill sites.

STEPPE EAGLE *A nipalensis* Large heavy build; heavy beak; dingy-white chin, may show rufous-buff splotch on nape; in flight, pale patch on rump, upperwings; in OH flight, **broad, long wings with noticeably splayed tips**; darker trailing-edge to wings; carpal-patches indistinct or absent; flight-feathers often barred; when gliding, **slight droop at carpals**.

(3) **IMPERIAL EAGLE** *A heliaca* **Diagnostic buff-yellow crown, nape**; indistinct white patches on scapulars; in OH flight, long, broad wings **splayed at tips**; when gliding/soaring, flattest-held wings than other Aquilas; seen at open areas, cultivation, creeks, marshes.

COMMON KESTREL *Falco tinnunculus*

14"

Slender, rufous and grey falcon, often hovering in mid-air

R/LM

PLUMAGE Rufous-chestnut above, spotted black; **grey crown, nape; grey tail**, with black tip; pale-buff below, streaked darker; in flight, rufous and grey above; in OH flight, pale underbody, **black tail-tip. Female:** Rufous-brown above, marked blackish; more **rusty, dark-barred tail**.

HABITS Often on roadside electric poles, wires, flying around cliff-faces in Shyd; **hovers in mid-air**, 10-30 m up; drops lower to check; pounces, legs outstretched to snatch prey (rodents, insects). **Call:** Shrill *kee-kee* or *kli-kli* with distinct trilling quality; more vocal when brdg (Feb-May).

Khopoli-Karjat
Murbad
Uran
Panvel
Alibaug-N,S
Shahpur
Wada
Manor
Aarey
Fairly common

*Breeds Shyd,
Matheran Range*

LAGGAR FALCON *Falco jugger*

18"

Dark-brown and white falcon

WV

PLUMAGE Deep ashy-brown above; at close range, **pale-rufous crown, dark moustachial stripes**; whitish cheeks; **whitish below, streaked darker on lower-breast, belly; in OH flight**, whitish body, **darker around flanks**, occ much-streaked breast, abdomen. **Juv:** Very heavily streaked below.

HABITS Solitary or pairs close by; settles on electric poles, bare treetops, tall buildings; strikes from vantage perch; seen attacking pigeons in S Mumbai.

Uran
Aarey
Panvel
Karjat
Wada
also occ
Thane Crk
S&C Mumbai
Uncommon

EURASIAN EAGLE OWL *Bubo bubo*

22-24"

Large, 'horned' owl of rocky areas

R

Alibaug-N
Shirsat
Wada
Gorai (once)
Uncommon

In recent years, small population in abandoned Dahisar Quarry (edge of SGNP)

PLUMAGE Tawny-buff and brown above, profusely-mottled/streaked; **conspicuous horn-like ear-tufts**; pale chin, throat; pale-buff below, **streaked breast, flanks**; feathered tarsus and **distinctive orangish-yellow eyes**.

HABITS Pairs or solitary; hides by day in rock-faces; occ basks early mornings. Call: **Diagnostic, deep, booming** *bu-booh* or *to-whoo* far-reaching call; occ snapping calls and shrieks.

GREY NIGHTJAR *Caprimulgus indicus*

11"

Cryptic-coloured, nocturnal bird

R

Most sites
Fairly common

PLUMAGE Grey or ashy-brown overall, **profusely-mottled, marked and vermiculated brown**, buff and black; white throat-patch, **small wing-patch and tips of outertail feathers**.

HABITS Solitary or several scattered in an area; spends day on ground, active from dusk; tight squatter, flying when almost trampled upon. Call: Diagnostic, somewhat deep, rapid *chucku-chucku*.

RELATED **INDIAN NIGHTJAR** *C asiaticus* Rufous-buff nuchal collar; *chuk-chuk-chuk-chkrru* notes rolling into one another. Fairly common.

PAINTED FRANCOLIN *Francolinus pictus*

12-13"

Profusely-
marked, skulking
ground bird.

Sexes differ

R

Wada
Manor
Shirsat
Murbad
Khopoli-Karjat
Shahpur
Uncommon

*Nos appear to
be declining*

PLUMAGE Blackish-brown overall, heavily-
mottled white; dull-rufous wash on wings; **pale-
chestnut face, supercilium, throat**; black
outertail feathers. Female: Pale-rufous sides of
face; **white throat**.

HABITS Secretive, skulking bird of cover; small
scattered coveys; difficult to flush. **Call:** Vocal
during rains; diagnostic, grating *khik-khee-khee-
khheeki*; occ birds in duet.

JUNGLE BUSH QUAIL *Perdicula asiatica*

7"

Plump, cryptic-
coloured quail
of heavy
undergrowth

R

Most sites
Fairly common

PLUMAGE Brown above, profusely-mottled black
and buff; **rufous-buff supercilium; rufous-
orange chin, throat**; dull-white below, finely
barred blackish-brown. Female: **Dull pinkish-
rufous below; rufous throat**.

HABITS Usually small coveys; rummages amid
leaf-litter, often along favoured paths; explodes
suddenly when almost stepped upon, scattering
with a *whirr* and faint chirping. **Call:** Trilling,
musical *wih-whiwhiwhiwhi* after dropping into
cover; male noisy when brdg (rains); also harsh
screams and chuckles.

BARRED BUTTONQUAIL *Turnix suscitator*

6"

Profusely-mottled, quail-like, secretive bird. Sexes differ

R/LM

Wada
Manor
Khopoli-Karjat
Vadhkal
Alibaug-N,S
Uncommon

Nest found near Kohoj

PLUMAGE Rufous-brown above, mottled black and buff; darker crown; **whitish chin; buff below, boldly barred blackish;** rufous-orange flanks, belly; in flight, pale-buff on wing-shoulders; greyish legs, feet. **Female:** Slightly larger, brighter rufous-buff below, with **diagnostic black throat, breast-centre.**

HABITS Pairs or few scattered in an area; secretive and elusive, occ emerging in clearings; flushed with difficulty; flies low. Call: Loud drumming of female (rains); also a soft but resonant *ghuu* or *hoon*.

ASHY WOODSWALLOW *Artamus fuscus*

7"

Dumpy, pale-grey bird of open tracts, swallow-like in flight

R

Shirsat
Manor
Wada
Alibaug-N,S
Vadhkal
occ Aarey,
Vikhroli, Panvel
Uncommon

Nos declined considerably since early-1990s

PLUMAGE **Slaty-grey,** darker on wings, tail; **dull grey-white below throat; short, square tail,** narrowly-tipped white; **OH flight,** pale underbody, **dark tail, flight-feathers;** bluish, conical beak. Looks swallow-like in flight, but heavier build, broader wings help to distinguish.

HABITS In palmyra-dotted open terrain; flies swallow-like or huddles tight on bare branches; usually a few around; hawks winged insects. Call: Quite vocal; harsh, nasal *chaeyk-chayk,* mostly in flight, occ a short song (Mar-Jun).

RED-WATTLED LAPWING *Vanellus indicus* 13"

PLUMAGE Olive-brown mantle, wings (slight bronze wash); **jet-black head, neck, upper-breast**; **white band** from behind eyes, **along neck-sides** to white underbody; **diagnostic bright-red facial wattles**; **in flight**, black and white tail. Long, yellowish legs.

HABITS Demonstrative and vocal; pairs or several around; often around water, occ in forest clearings. **Call**: Diagnostic loud *tit-re-te-tew* call (best interpreted '*did-he-do-it*'); often calls during night; various alarm-notes when disturbed.

Highly vocal, long-legged bird, usually close to water
R

All sites
occ Kalina, Juhu airfield
Fairly common

YELLOW-WATTLED LAPWING *V malabaricus* 11"

PLUMAGE Sandy-brown above; **black cap**, bordered below, white stripe; **diagnostic yellow facial-wattles**; white below breast; **in flight** prominent **white band on wings**; white tail with black terminal band. Long yellow legs.

HABITS Pairs usually close by; unobtrusive, often overlooked; moves slowly, cautiously. **Call**: A low *t-witl*, repeated several times, especially when alarmed; occ a harsh note; overall much quieter than Red-wattled.

(inset) Brown and white bird of dry, open areas
R

Khopoli
Wada
Manor
Uran
Uncommon

Declined much since early-1990s; found brdg Aksa-Madh up to 1992

LAUGHING DOVE *Streptopelia senegalensis*

10"

Small, pink-brown dove with grey and black on wings

R/LM

♪

Uran
Khopoli-Karjat
Murbad
Wada
Manor
Uncommon

*Nest found
near Uran*

PLUMAGE Sandy-brown above; lilac-pink head, neck; **diagnostic black and rufous-buff 'chess-board' on upper-breast**; grey on wing-shoulders; pinkish-brown breast; **in flight, prominent black wing-tips, grey wing-patches.**

HABITS Pairs or solitary; occ few scattered around; also gleans with Spotted Dove.
Call: Distinctive soft, pleasant *croo-do-dodoo-du.*

RELATED RED COLLARED DOVE *S tranquebarica*
Deep-grey head, throat; vinaceous-red mantle; black hind-neck collar; rolling call. Uncommon.

SPOTTED DOVE *Streptopelia chinensis*

12"

Pale-brownish dove, spotted paler above

R

♪ ● ●

All sites
Common

PLUMAGE Earthy pinkish-brown above; pale feather-edges give **spotted appearance**; black and white 'chess-board' on hind-neck; dull vinous-brown below; **in flight, dark flight-feathers**, grey patch on wing-shoulders; broad, **white tip to outertail feathers.**

HABITS Solitary or pairs; occ several around; gleans on roads, cart-tracks, fields; settles in leafy trees. **Call: Diagnostic soft, 3-noted** *croo-croo-croo* from perch.

BLACK DRONGO   *Dicrurus macrocercus*

11"

Slender, black
bird with
forked tail

R

All sites
occ S&C Mumbai
Common

PLUMAGE **Jet-black**, with **variable gloss;
reddish eyes; diagnostic tail, long, deeply-
forked.** Juv: Brown wash in plumage; white
speckling on abdomen.

HABITS Familiar bird of open terrain, perched
on telegraph wires, bush-tops; hawks winged
insects; attends to grazing cattle, grass-cutters,
fires; with other birds regularly on landfills and
flowering trees. Call: Distinctive 2-noted
che-chwae or *tchi-tiu*; short trilling song (Apr-Jul).

PIED CUCKOO   *Clamator jacobinus*

13"

Long-tailed,
crested, black
and white bird

BV

Most sites
occ S&C Mumbai
Fairly common

PLUMAGE **Jet-black above**, with conspicuous
crest; **white wing-patch, tail-tip,** more
prominent in flight; white underbody.
Juv: (Aug-Dec) Pale sooty-brown and dull-white.

HABITS Widely regarded as a harbinger of
SW monsoon; pairs or solitary; small bands upon
arrival (mid/late-May), when much mobbed by
Mumbai's House Crow; often feeds on ground.
Call: Most vocal late-May-Jul; loud, metallic
plew-piu or *plew-piu-peeu* chiefly in flight,
occ on perch.

GREATER COUCAL *Centropus sinensis*

19"

Long-tailed, skulking, black and chestnut bird

R

♪ ● ●

Most sites also occ S&C Mumbai
Fairly common

PLUMAGE Blackish overall, with purplish-blue gloss; **diagnostic chestnut wings. Juv:** Dark-brownish, scalloped paler; dingy-white below, barred.

HABITS A non-parasitic cuckoo; keeps to thick growth, both in bush and in leafy branches; frequently emerges on ground; slow, sluggish movements; weak, low flight, never flying far. **Call:** Diagnostic, loud, deep, somewhat-booming *koop-koop*, often several times at a stretch; occ a harsh, grating cry.

BLUE-FACED MALKOHA *Phaenicophaeus viridirostris*

16"

Dull-green, skulking bird with very long, graduated tail

R

♪ ●

Alibaug-S Wada Khopoli
Uncommon

PLUMAGE **Greyish-green above;** much paler below; **diagnostic bright-green beak,** bluish bare patch around eye; **long, graduated tail, tipped white.**

HABITS Keeps to low scrub; occ forest sites (Phansad); sneaks and climbs about branches, rarely descending to ground; solitary or pairs; slow, arduous-looking flight. **Call:** Occ a throaty *khrrr*.

ASIAN PALM SWIFT *Cypsiurus balasiensis*

5"

Fork-tailed bird incessantly flying around palmyras

R

PLUMAGE Sooty-brown above, darker on wings, tail; pale ashy-brown below, duller on chin, throat; slender, **deeply-forked tail** (occ opened in flight).

All sites also occ S&C, suburban Mumbai **Common**

HABIT Familiar over palmyra-dotted country; occ forest; usually several hawking insects; nests and settles on underside of palmyra fronds. **Call:** Faint but shrill 3-noted *ti-ti-chee* in flight.

ALPINE SWIFT *Tachymarptis melba*

9"

Large, brown and white swift of mountain country

R/LM

PLUMAGE Sooty-brown above; **in OH flight, diagnostic white chin, throat, belly; brown breast-band, abdomen, undertail-coverts**; long, sickle-shaped, pointed wings.

Khopoli-Karjat also occ KBS, Kanheri (SGNP), Kohoj **Uncommon**

HABITS A wild bird in the true sense; loose flocks fly fast and erratic, screaming and tumbling around cliffs, over mountainous country; suddenly appear briefly over an area; skim over water surface to drink. **Call:** Trilling *chrrrr-chee-chee* screams in flight.

GREEN BEE-EATER *Merops orientalis*

7-8"

Slender, greenish bird of open tracts

R/LM

All sites also S&C Mumbai

Common

PLUMAGE Grass-green overall; **pale golden-ferruginous sheen on crown, nape**; black eye-stripe; blue-green throat, bordered by **fine black gorget; elongated central tail-feathers.**
Juv: Pale-green crown; pale-yellow throat.

HABITS Usually several around; perches on telegraph wires, trees, bush-tops; hawks insects in flight; occ attends to grazing cattle; also in city parks, forest-edges. Call: Cheerful, twittering *ttree-tree* mostly in flight.

BLUE-TAILED BEE-EATER *Merops philippinus*

10"

Slender, greenish bird, often around water

PM

Uran
Talzan
Gorai
Manor
Shirsat
Alibaug-N
Uncommon

Seldom stays for many days in an area

PLUMAGE Green above; **broad black eye-stripe,** bordered above and below with blue; **verditer-blue rump, tail, elongated central tail-feathers;** chestnut throat; green below, with slight bluish wash. Juv: Lacks long central tail-feathers.

HABITS Several around water, forest-edges.
Call: Distinctive; somewhat rolling *tche-tcheerp* or *tteerrp* in flight; louder than Green's.

RELATED BLUE-CHEEKED BEE-EATER *M persicus*
Conspicuous bluish ear-coverts; greenish rump, tail; less common than Blue-tailed. Scarce.

INDIAN ROLLER *Coracias benghalensis*

13"

Striking, heavy bird revealing bright blue in flight

LM/WV

PLUMAGE Dull greenish-brown above, blue-green crown; white streaks on face-sides, throat; **diagnostic bright-turquoise and dark-blue wings, tail**; pale-vinous breast; dull-blue below.

HABITS Occ forest-edges; often on telegraph poles, wires; inconspicuous when perched; leisurely flight; sometimes hawks insects.
Call: Occ harsh *khaak*.

Most sites also occ S&C, suburban Mumbai
Fairly common

COMMON HOOPOE *Upupa epops*

12"

Fawn-coloured bird with black and white wings and tail

WV

PLUMAGE **Fawn-coloured overall** (pinkish-buff); **broad, fan-shaped crest, tipped black; diagnostic black and white in wings and tail,** seen at rest and in flight; rounded-wings; long, curved, slender beak.

HABITS Unobtrusive here; pairs usually close by; occ several together; digs, probes on ground with long beak; often on coastal fallow lands.
Call: An occ harsh, grating call.

Gorai
Alibaug-N,S
Khopoli-Karjat
Shirsat
Wada
Manor
also occ S&C, suburban Mumbai
Fairly common

ASHY-CROWNED SPARROW LARK *Eremopterix grisea*

5"

Tiny ground-bird with finch-like beak. Sexes differ

R/LM

Shirsat
Uran
Vikhroli
Kalyan
Vadhkal
Alibaug-N,S
Manor
Shahpur
Fairly common

PLUMAGE Pale ashy-brown above, greyer on crown; whitish cheeks; **blackish-brown underbody**; dull-white on outertail feathers. Thick, finch-like beak. **Female:** Browner above, with slight grey wash; **pale-rufous below**.

HABITS Stony open lands, mudflats, cultivation; quite sociable, often even when brdg (Dec-Jun; sporadically Oct-Nov); squats tight. Call: Trilling display-song of courting male; occ sings on ground; periodically shrill, long-drawn *sweeesh*, especially on descent or dive.

RUFOUS-TAILED LARK *Ammomanes phoenicurus*

6-7"

Thickset, brown and rufous bird of open areas

R/LM

Kalyan
Shirsat
Uran
Manor
Wada
Vadhkal
Shahpur
Vikhroli
occ creeksides
Fairly common

PLUMAGE Darkish-brown above, edged paler on wing-feathers; buff or pale-rufous supercilium; **diagnostic bright-rufous tail with dark terminal band**; dull-rufous below, streaked darker on throat, breast.

HABITS Pairs or small, loose bands; occ on telegraph wires; perches on bush-tops; seen in ploughed fields, short grass, stony terrain, mudflats. Call: Melodious trilling song of male during display-flight; sometimes sings on exposed perch (Mar-Jun); a medley of chirping notes punctuated by rich, mellow notes.

MALABAR LARK *Galerida malabarica*

6-7"

Rufous-brown, streaked bird with prominent crest

R

PLUMAGE Rufous-brown above, profusely-streaked; **diagnostic** upstanding crest; **pale-rufous outertail feathers**; whitish below, with pale tawny-buff wash; **conspicuous, dark-streaked breast.**

HABITS Grassy marsh-edges, hillsides, fields, mudflats; usually pairs in vicinity, sometimes scattered flocks. Call: Pleasant-sounding *chew-tchee-tchu*; an occ sharp *quee-tchi*; short, rambling song of male, often interspersed with ordinary call-notes; calls on ground and during soaring flight.

Kalyan
Uran
Shirsat
Panvel
Vikhroli
Karjat
Alibaug-N
Murbad
Uncommon

ORIENTAL SKYLARK *Alauda gulgula*

6"

Streaked, brownish bird with short crest

R/LM

PLUMAGE Mostly pale-fulvous above, streaked darker; **short, roundish crest**; pale supercilium; **dull-rufous primaries** (also seen when settled); pale-buff outertail feathers; buffy-white below, streaked throat, breast.

HABITS Grassy fallow lands, mudflats, fields; usually pairs; small gatherings during winter. Call: A soft *chirr-upp*; occ *tszeeb*; male song (Mar-Jun; occ Sep-Oct) a lengthy outpouring of fairly high-pitched, musical phrases; **sings in spectacular display-flight**, rising and dropping; intermittently hovers; may sing on perch.

Uran
Kalyan
Shirsat
Vadhkal
Alibaug-N
Vikhroli
also occ Kalina,
Juhu airfield
Uncommon

GREATER SHORT-TOED LARK *Calandrella brachydactyla*

6"

Gregarious,
streaked,
sandy-buff and
white bird

WV

Uran
Vadhkal
Shirsat
Kalyan
Vikhroli
Panvel

Fairly common

*Quite abundant
some years*

PLUMAGE Sandy-brown above (may show dull-tawny wash), streaked darker; **pale-white supercilium, outertail feathers**; whitish below, very faintly-streaked breast-sides; **distinctive dark patch on neck-sides.**

HABITS Gregarious; often congregates at certain localities, especially Uran, Bhandup; seen in mudflats, grassy, stony margins of wetlands, cultivation. **Call:** Occ short *chi-chrrp* in flight.

DUSKY CRAG MARTIN *Hirundo concolor*

5"

Small, sooty-brown bird flying around cliffs, old buildings

R

Wada
Manor
Murbad
Khopoli-Karjat
Shahpur
also S&C Mumbai

Fairly common

PLUMAGE Uniform deep sooty-brown above; white-spotted tail-tip, not easily seen; in OH flight, dark underbody; **very slight notch in short tail.**

HABITS Cliff-sides, ruins, occ with swallows, swifts; hawks insects; rests and breeds on rock-faces, roof ledges. **Call:** Occ a faint, rapid *chit-chit* in flight.

RELATED EURASIAN CRAG MARTIN *H rupestris* WV Paler overall; in flight very **pale underbody**, dark undertail; occ urban areas. Uncommon.

RED-RUMPED SWALLOW *Hirundo daurica*

8"

Swallow with chestnut rump and deeply-forked tail

R/LM/WV

PLUMAGE Dark metallic-blue above; **diagnostic rufous-chestnut rump, collar**; pale-buff below, finely-streaked; **OH flight**, pale underbody, **deeply-forked (dark) tail**.

Most sites also S&C Mumbai
Common
(few breed)

HABITS Settles on telegraph wires; often amid habitation; gregarious in winter; wheels and banks in acrobatic flight. **Call:** A wistful *cserr* note in flight; pleasant twittering song of brdg male (rare in Mumbai proper).

BARN SWALLOW *Hirundo rustica*

8"

Fork-tailed swallow with chestnut throat

WV

PLUMAGE Dark metallic-blue above; **diagnostic chestnut-red forehead, throat**; **dark band across upper-breast**; unmarked whitish below; **deeply-forked tail** (partly white), with elongated outer feathers. **Juv:** Lacks long tail-streamers.

Most sites also S&C Mumbai
Common

HABITS Open areas, vicinity of wetlands, habitation; gregarious; large numbers roost in reed beds, creeks; perch on overhead wires. **Call:** Sharp, rapid *tchswee* in flight.

LONG-TAILED SHRIKE *Lanius schach*

10"

Long-tailed, noisy, grey and rufous bird

WV

♪ ●

All sites also occ S&C Mumbai
Common

Breeds Malshej, Lonavala-Khandala

PLUMAGE Broad, black eye-stripe; pale-grey crown, upper back merge into **rufous lower back**, **rump**; blackish wings with small, white patch; **long, blackish tail with rufous outer feathers**; white below, with **dull-rufous wash on flanks**, breast-sides. **Juv:** More rufous-brown above, speckled.

HABITS Highly vocal on arrival (early-Sep); solitary, but few invariably scattered around; swoops on prey from perch. **Call: Diagnostic, harsh, screaming calls;** soft melodious song of brdg male (heard Talzan).

BAY-BACKED SHRIKE *Lanius vittatus*

7"

Grey and maroon bird with black forehead and eye-stripe

WV

●

Manor
Wada
Kalyan
Alibaug-N,S
Panvel
also occ
Aarey, SGNP
Uncommon

PLUMAGE Diagnostic black band across forehead through eyes; grey crown, nape; **chestnut-maroon mantle; white wing-mirrors;** in flight, black and white wings, tail, **whitish rump**; white below, with pale-fulvous wash on breast, darker on flanks.

HABITS Occ forest- and creek-edge; often solitary; may linger in a locality for several days. **Call:** Harsh, grating *khae* and an occ *chweurr-chweurr*.

BROWN SHRIKE *Lanius cristatus*

7-8"

Rufous-tailed, pale-brown bird with black eye-stripe

LM/WV

PLUMAGE **Pale-brown above**, with very slight rufous wash; **white supercilium**; broad, black eye-stripe; **rufous-brown tail**; white chin, throat; pale buff-white below. Juv: Scalloped above.

HABITS Solitary or pairs; occ hunts insects until after dusk. Call: Harsh *chrr-rri* and *khae* with a distinctly chiding tone.

RLATED **RUFOUS-TAILED SHRIKE** *L isabellinus* WV/PM Sandy-brown mantle; more rufous crown, rump and tail; **small white wing-patch**; sighted Uran, Khopoli. Uncommon.

Uran
Alibaug-N
Manor
Wada
Kalyan
Aarey
Panvel
Uncommon

INDIAN PITTA *Pitta brachyura*

7-8"

Colourful, plump, stub-tailed bird of undergrowth

PM

Intermittently most sites
Regularly urban areas
Uncommon

PLUMAGE **Broad, black eye-stripe up to nape; green back, wings; blue in wings**, lower-back, tail; white chin, throat; fulvous below; **crimson lower-abdomen, undertail-coverts**; in flight, white patch near wing-tips.

HABITS Spends much time on ground, rummaging for insects; flies into trees upon alarm; pairs usually close by; molested by House Crow in urban areas. Call: Distinctive; 2-noted *wheee-peu* whistle; frequently calls.

CHESTNUT-TAILED STARLING *Sturnus malabaricus*

8"

Arboreal, silvery-grey and rufous bird

LM/PM

♪ ●

Most sites
Fairly common

PLUMAGE Silvery grey-brown above; **whitish shaft-streaks on paler head**; grey-white throat, **rufous-brown below; pale-blue eyes.**

HABITS Largely arboreal; small parties, often with other birds on flowering, fruiting trees, even amid habitation; arrives early-Sep; periodically vanishes to reappear Dec/Jan. Call: Whistling *krreep*; various screeching notes.

RELATED WHITE-HEADED RACE *blythii* With whiter head, breast; occ Sep-Oct; urban areas, open country. Uncommon.

JUNGLE MYNA *Acridotheres fuscus*

9"

Like Common Myna but without yellow around eye

LM/R

♪ ●

Uran
Karjat
Manor
Panvel
Alibaug-N,S
also occ KBS,
Tungar

Uncommon

PLUMAGE At a glance quite similar to Common Myna; dark grey-brown overall; **distinctive tuft of feathers on forehead; pale-grey eyes; lacks yellow skin around eye**; white in wings, tail. Juv: **Browner**; slighter, often indistinct tuft of forehead feathers.

HABITS Cultivation, forest-edge, habitation; small parties; around cattle or feeding on ground; also visits flowering trees; less confiding than Common Myna, hence often overlooked. Call: Various chuckling, screaming notes.

ROSY STARLING *Sturnus roseus*

9"

Raucous,
rose-pink and
black bird

WV

PLUMAGE (Sep and late-Mar/early-Apr) **Rich rosy-pink mantle, rump, underbody below breast; glossy-black head, bushy crest**; black wings, tail. Duller and drab through winter. Juv: Dull-brown; lacks crest.

HABITS Highly gregarious and clamorous; wanders locally, **reappearing in abundance with flowering of Indian Coral** (Feb-Mar); chiefly insectivorous; feeds on ground, landfill sites; restive and querulous. **Call:** Extremely noisy; medley of chattering screams and musical notes.

Most sites
also S&C Mumbai
Common

ASIAN PIED STARLING *Sturnus contra*

9"

Black and white
vocal bird

R

PLUMAGE Pied. Black above incl wings, tail; **whitish around eyes; white wing-patch**, rump, underbody below breast; **orangish orbital-patch**; yellowish beak, legs.

HABITS Commonly amid habitation, usually small bands; prefers damp localities, vicinity of cattle-sheds. **Call:** Distinctive; rich and varied notes, mix of harsh and musical screams, whistles; short warbling song (May-Aug).

Most sites
Fairly common

*Not endemic;
escaped cage-birds
first settled mid-
1900s in suburban
Mumbai, Thane*

WHITE-EARED BULBUL *Pycnonotus leucotis*

8"

Sprightly, brown
bird with white
cheek-patch

R

♪

All creeksides
Vikhroli
Uran
Navi Mumbai
Manor
Fairly common

PLUMAGE Ashy-brown above; **black head**; slight,
rounded crest; **diagnostic white ear-coverts**;
pale-buff below; conspicuous **yellow vent**;
darker **tail, tipped white** on all but central pair
of feathers.

HABITS Occ mangrove creeks; pairs or small
bands; infrequently on flowering trees; descends
on ground to pick ants, termites. Call: Cheerful,
3-5-noted whistle; also harsh alarm-notes.

RED-VENTED BULBUL *Pycnonotus cafer*

8"

Dark, sooty-
brown bird with
red undertail

R

♪ ● ●

All sites
Urban areas
Common

PLUMAGE **Jet-black head**, small, flat crest;
profusely scaly-patterned sooty-brown overall,
paler below; white lower-back (in flight);
diagnostic bright-crimson vent; white tips to
all but central tail-feathers.

HABITS Keeps to bush and middle storey;
usually several around; a must in every mixed
bird party; descends to ground to pick ants;
noisy, cheery and querulous. Call: Distinctive
2-4-noted, cheery whistling call; grating calls
when disturbed or alarmed.

YELLOW-EYED BABBLER *Chrysomma sinense*

7"

Long-tailed rufous and white bird of bush growth

R

PLUMAGE Rich rufous-brown above, brighter cinnamon-rufous on wings; **diagnostic orangish eye-rim, yellow eyes**; long, graduated tail; **unstreaked white throat, breast**; fulvous below. Blackish beak, orange-yellow legs.

HABITS Skulks in bush, tall grass; pairs or 3-5 birds; clambers atop a bush; weak, low flight across paths, clearings. **Call:** Diagnostic (May-Aug); a 5-6-noted, melodious *tchwe-checha-tchi-whee-chu*, with accent on penultimate note; also a loud *cheep-cheep*.

Aarey
Kalyan
Vikhroli
Uran
Panvel
Vadhkal
Navi Mumbai
Talzan
Fairly common

Declining since early-1990s

ZITTING CISTICOLA *Cisticola juncidis*

4"

Tiny, short-tailed, streaked bird of grassy areas

R/LM

PLUMAGE Fulvous above, boldly-streaked; plain rufous rump; pale supercilium; **short tail**, outer feathers tipped white; **unstreaked, pale-buff below**. Paler in winter, when crown more profusely streaked.

HABITS Usually several scattered on open grassy terrain; skulks in vegetation; jerky flight; most active Jun-Oct. **Call:** Distinctive; surprisingly far-reaching, sharp *zit-zzit*, mostly in flight; seldom when settled.

Kalyan
Uran
Vadhkal
Malvani
Vikhroli
Talzan
Shirsat
Alibaug-N,S
Panvel
also occ
S&C Mumbai
Fairly common

GREY-BREASTED PRINIA *Prinia hodgsonii*

4-5"

Long-tailed, ashy-brown bird of bush growth

R

Most sites
Common

Rapidly expanding species post-1980s

PLUMAGE BRDG: (rains) Rich ashy-grey above, browner on wings; whitish below with **diagnostic broad, pale-grey breast-band.**
NON BRDG: Browner above; often pale supercilium; whitish tips to outertail feathers

HABITS Often along forest-edges; pairs or several usually close by; active, vocal. **Call:** Most vocal May-Sep; distinctive soft, twittering song; often calls from high perch; occ a *chwirrrrr* call.

PLAIN PRINIA *Prinia inornata*

5"

Pale-brown bird of tall grass and scrub

R

Uran
Talzan
Shirsat
Kalyan
Murbad
Alibaug-N
Panvel
also MB marshes
Fairly common

PLUMAGE BRDG: (May-Sep) Dull earthy-brown above; **buff-white supercilium;** pale-whitish below. **NON BRDG:** Dark-brown above, with slight rufous wash.

HABITS Several scattered over an area; skulks in vegetation; often overlooked during dry season. **Call:** Distinctive song; wheezy, chirring and grasshopper-like in tone; also a low *paee-pee*, occ interspersed with a jarring *grrik* sound.

ASHY PRINIA *Prinia socialis*

5"

Long-tailed, dark-ashy and buff bird of vegetation

R

PLUMAGE BRDG: (Apr-Oct) **Slaty-grey crown, upper-back; rufous-brown wings, tail (tipped white);** tawny-buff below. **NON BRDG: Slaty-grey largely on crown;** more rufous-brown above; may show short, pale supercilium.

HABITS Clambers amid low vegetation, commonly around habitation; solitary or pairs; low, weak flight. **Call:** Distinctive *pae-pae*, quite nasal in tone; Tailorbird-like song of male, a loud, cheery *jivee-jivee*; snapping sound when alarmed, usually in jumpy, low flight.

Most sites
Urban areas
Common

COMMON CHIFFCHAFF *Phylloscopus collybita*

4-5"

Small, dull-coloured bird

WV

PLUMAGE Dull-brown, with variable greyish tinge; may show slight olivish on wings and tail; **pale supercilium;** dingy-white below; **blackish legs, beak.**

HABITS Occ forest, forest-edges; solitary or 2-3 birds in an area; skulks in bush, occ emerging in open. **Call:** Soft *twueet*; occ a soft 2-noted call.

Aarey
Khopoli
Alibaug-N,S
Wada
occ Vikhroli,
Talzan
also occ SGNP
Uncommon

BOOTED WARBLER *Hippolais caligata*

5"

Tiny, skulking
pale-brownish
bird

WV

Most sites
occ creeksides
Fairly common

PLUMAGE Pale-brown above; **pale supercilium**, sometimes indistinct; may show some white on outertail feathers; whitish below, often with pale-buff on breast, flanks; **lacks wing-bar.**

HABITS Often solitary, sometimes several around; skulks in low vegetation and middle storey. Call: A soft, typically tongue-clicking *tchak-tchak*; occ a faint *churr*.

RELATED BLYTH'S REED WARBLER *Acrocephalus dumetorum* More greyish-olive above; short, supercilium; fairly loud *tchak*. Fairly common.

TICKELL'S LEAF WARBLER *Phylloscopus affinis*

4"

Tiny, olive-green
and yellow,
skulking bird

WV

Murbad
Karjat
Alibaug-N.S
Aarey
Manor
Wada
Fairly common

PLUMAGE Dull-greenish above (may have brownish wash); **distinctive yellow supercilium**; yellow below, brighter on throat, breast.

HABITS Skulks in bush and secondary growth, intermittently ascending into higher branches. Call: A quickly-uttered *tchk-chuk*.

RELATED SULPHUR-BELLIED WARBLER *P griseolus* Darker, greyer above, with greenish tinge; yellow supercilium; dingy-yellow below; skulks; ruins, rocky areas; sighted SGNP fringes, Aarey, KBS, Bassein Fort. Uncommon.

BLUETHROAT *Luscinia svecica*

6"

Brownish bird of damp vegetation. Sexes differ

WV

●

PLUMAGE Drab-brown above; **white supercilium; rufous-chestnut in tail; blue, rufous and black throat, breast;** more extensive blue on arrival (early-Oct) and occ late-Mar, often with chestnut spot in centre. **Female: Lacks blue on throat;** brown spotting on breast.

HABITS Wary; keeps to damp cover, often on creeksides; usually several around, emerging often at edge of cover. **Call:** Occ a harsh *charrr*, possibly an alarm-note.

Uran
Panvel
Manor
Shirsat
Vikhroli
occ MNP,
S Mumbai,
Elephanta
Fairly common

BLACK REDSTART *Phoenicurus ochruros*

6"

Grey-black bird with shivering, rusty tail. Sexes differ

WV

●

PLUMAGE Sooty-black above; may show faint-white on forehead; **rusty-rufous rump, outertail feathers; black throat, upper-breast; rufous-orange below. Female:** Slaty-brown above; **rufous rump, outertail feathers.**

HABITS Largely open areas, groves; solitary or pairs; makes short sallies from bush-tops, trees, overhead wires; **shivers tail often;** regularly descends to ground to pick insects. **Call:** A faint *whee-ditdic*, sometimes preceded by a soft *fheet*.

Manor
Wada
Murbad
Kalyan
Khopoli
Navi Mumbai
Shahpur
Alibaug-N,S
occ urban areas
Uncommon

COMMON STONECHAT *Saxicola torquata*

5"

Brownish-black and rufous bird of open terrain. Sexes differ

WV

Most sites occ Juhu airfield, Bhavan's campus, Kalina, Racecourse
Fairly common

PLUMAGE Male: **(on arrival, early-Oct) Blackish above; white half-collar, rump. WINTER:** Brownish-black above, feathers edged fulvous; white wing-stripe; **rufous-chestnut breast** fades to dull-buff below. Female: Brown above, **streaked**; small white wing-patch; buff chin, throat; dull rufous-orange below.

HABITS Often marsh-edges; solitary, pairs or several along length of road; perches on stones, poles, bush-tops; frequently alights on ground. Call: Occ soft but rapid *tsic-tsak*; and a low clicking sound.

DESERT WHEATEAR *Oenanthe deserti*

6"

Unobtrusive, sandy-brown bird of open terrain

WV

Uran
Manor
Shirsat
Panvel
Navi Mumbai
Malvani
occ creeksides
Uncommon

PLUMAGE Sandy-brown overall; **darker about face, chin, throat**; dark wings; **black tail; dull-white rump**, uppertail-coverts. Occ retains brdg plumage Oct-Nov, when jet-black face-sides, throat, wings. Female: **Duller overall**; browner where male is black.

HABITS Open, barren areas; occ marsh, creeksides; difficult to spot; mostly hops on ground; occ flies up to catch insects. Call: Occ a faint *tse-tchet*.

INDIAN ROBIN *Saxicoloides fulicata*

7"

Blackish bird with cocked tail and white in wings. Sexes differ

R

Most sites
Fairly common

PLUMAGE Blackish above, with variable gloss; **white shoulder-patch; chestnut vent, abdomen-centre** (best seen when tail cocked). Female: Dark-brown above, paler below, chestnut vent; **lacks white in wings.**

HABITS Sometimes around habitation; pairs usually close by; hops on ground, head held high, tail often cocked. **Call:** Distinctive; drawn-out *schweech*; occ a harsh alarm-note; brdg male (Mar-Aug) has short, trilling song.

PIED BUSHCHAT *Saxicola caprata*

5"

Small, black and white bird of open areas. Sexes differ

R/WV

Murbad
Karjat
Shahpur
Uncommon
(few breed Shyd)

PLUMAGE **Jet-black above, below; white wing-patch;** white rump, abdomen. Female: Dull-brown above; **rufous rump; dark tail;** pale-fulvous below, more rufous towards flanks.

HABITS Occ forest-edge; often solitary; has favourite exposed perches; often descends to ground; jerks tail. **Call:** A chipping 2-noted call; brdg male (Mar-Jul) has short, melodious song.

BLUE ROCK THRUSH *Monticola solitarius*

9"

Dull-plumaged bird of open, rocky areas

WV

Manor
Wada
Karjat
Khopoli
also occ SGNP
Uncommon

Occ on high-rise bldgs in suburban Mumbai

PLUMAGE **Bluish overall**, with distinctly **dull tone**; brighter about head; brown wash on wings, tail. **Female:** Duller; **slaty-brown above**, scaly-patterned and speckled; pale-buff below.

HABITS Chiefly open, rocky areas; occ suburban areas; shy and wary; solitary but another bird may not be far; sits still, periodically descending to ground to pick insects; often has favoured spots.

PADDYFIELD PIPIT *Anthus rufulus*

6"

Slender, brown, streaked bird of open ground

R

Uran
Kalyan
Vikhroli
Shirsat
Vadhkal
Alibaug-N
occ Kalina,
Juhu airfield,
Vihar Lk edges
Fairly common

PLUMAGE **Tawny above, broadly-streaked**; pale stripe over eye; dark spotting along bend of wings (coverts) **white in outertail feathers**; whitish and pale-fulvous below, **streaked breast**.

HABITS Pairs close by; small bands possible in winter; occ marsh-edges. **Call:** Faint, somewhat plaintive *tssip* or *tseep*; twittering display-song of brdg male (Mar-Aug).

TREE PIPIT *Anthus trivialis*

6"

Slender, streaked, brownish bird, running on ground

WV

PLUMAGE **Buff-brown above** (with pale olive-grey wash), **streaked darker;** pale-buff supercilium; indistinct moustachial stripe; **whitish outertail feathers;** pale-buff below, **boldly streaked darker on breast**, flanks.

HABITS Forest-edges, low hillsides; usually loose flocks; flies into trees if disturbed. **Call:** Soft *tseep* or *tseeze*, often when flying into a tree.

RELATED **OLIVE-BACKED PIPIT** *A hodgsoni* **Olivish-green wash above**; whitish supercilium; broadly-streaked breast, flanks; sighted Karjat. Uncommon.

Murbad
Wada
Khopoli-Karjat
Alibaug-N,S
Navi Mumbai
Uncommon

BAYA WEAVER *Ploceus philippinus*

6"

Yellow and brown bird, renowned for its nest. Sexes differ

R/LM

PLUMAGE Brdg Male: **(May-Sep) Bright-yellow and dark-brown head;** streaked buff and brownish above; **diagnostic bright-yellow breast.** Female: Fulvous above, streaked darker; buff supercilium. Non Brdg Male: Like female, but may show yellow wash, variably streaked.

HABITS Suddenly erupts into view with foremost monsoon winds; sociable and noisy; best-known for its remarkable nest. **Call:** Distinctive; highly vocal when brdg; males constantly utter high-pitched, wheezy whistles and screechy notes.

Most sites occ suburban areas
Fairly common

Declining in immediate vicinity of Mumbai

RED AVADAVAT   *Amandava amandava*

4"

Tiny, reddish finch of damp grassy areas. Sexes differ

R/LM

Uran
Malvani
Vikhroli
Aarey
Panvel
Vadhkal
Alibaug-N,S
Talzan
Kalyan
Uncommon

PLUMAGE Brdg Male: (May-Sep) **Deep crimson-brown above**; dark-brown wings, tail; deep-crimson below; **diagnostic white spotting** on wings, flanks, breast-sides. **Female:** Brown above, with **black lores**; white spotting on dark wings; **crimson rump**; pale-buff below. **Non brdg Male:** Like female but dull-grey throat.

HABITS Prefers damp grassland, scrub; small bands during monsoon. **Call:** Sharp chirping notes, usually in low flight; brdg male has shrill, twittering song.

INDIAN SILVERBILL   *Lonchura malabarica*

4-5"

Pale-brown and white bird with pointed tail

R/LM

Uran
Vikhroli
Karjat
Panvel
Vadhkal
Alibaug-N
Shirsat
also occ
S&C Mumbai
Fairly common

PLUMAGE Pale-brown above; **white rump; dark wings, pointed tail**; pale-buff below, often lightly marked on flanks; **slaty-blue, greyish conical beak.**

HABITS Sometimes in dry terrain; usually several together; may feed with other munias, buntings, on ground, mud roads; observed roosting in abandoned Baya Weaver nests. **Call:** Occ *chrrp*; not very vocal.

WHITE-RUMPED MUNIA *Lonchura striata*

4"

Tiny blackish-brown and white bird

R/LM

PLUMAGE Deep blackish-brown head, wings and tail; **diagnostic white rump**; dark-brown mantle, faintly streaked paler (shaft-streaks), seen close range; **dark, pointed tail**; **blackish-brown throat, breast**; white below.

HABITS Small bands, either by themselves or with other munias at feeding sites; may roost with wagtails (sighted Talzan). **Call:** Occ a soft, plaintive *tseep* and a weak twitter.

Uran
Navi Mumbai
Vadhkal
Kalyan
Malvani
Talzan
Wada
also occ SGNP
Fairly common

SCALY-BREASTED MUNIA *Lonchura punctulata*

5"

Chocolate and white bird, speckled dark below

R/LM

PLUMAGE Chestnut-brown face-sides, throat, upper-breast; coffee-brown above; uppertail-coverts; **diagnostic blackish-brown and white speckled below breast**.

HABITS Sometimes forest-edges, around habitation; feeds with other weavers, munias and buntings. **Call:** 2-noted, somewhat snappish *kittee-kitee*, occ in flight; a faint *tchirrrp*, sometimes around nest.

Vikhroli
Aarey
Talzan
Uran
Panvel
Shirsat
occ Esselworld,
Juhu airfield
Fairly common

BLACK-HEADED MUNIA *Lonchura malacca*

4"

Small, chestnut and black bird with conical beak

R/LM

Vikhroli
Uran
Karjat
Alibaug-N
Kalyan
Malvani
Navi Mumbai
Murbad
suburban
Mumbai
Uncommon

PLUMAGE Rufous-brown above, with **jet-black head, throat, breast, belly-centre and undertail**; white abdomen, flanks. **Juv:** (seen Aug-Nov) Pale-brown above, darker on forehead, wings; pale-buff below.

HABITS Small bands on tall grassland, scrub, usually where damp; small gatherings with other munias to feed on ground; sighted around Black-breasted Weaver nests in Uran. **Call:** A soft *chrrp* in flight; occ also a plaintive *tsik*.

COMMON ROSEFINCH *Carpodacus erythrinus*

6"

Crimson-rose and brown bird. Sexes differ

WV

Karjat
Aarey
Murbad
Alibaug-N,S
Manor
also occ MNP,
SGNP, KBS,
Phansad
Uncommon

PLUMAGE Crimson crown, rump; brownish mantle, wings have crimson wash and fulvous margins to feathers; **crimson throat, breast** fade into **rosy-white below. Female:** Pale **olive-brown above, streaked;** pale wing-bars; dull-white below, **streaked breast.**

HABITS Groves, open forest; feeds in low, standing crop and on berries in leafy trees; visits flowering plants, incl Paper Flower climber and Lantana; often small, loose bands (early Mar-); sometimes basks on high branches. **Call:** Occ

BLACK-HEADED BUNTING *Emberiza melanocephala*

7"

Yellow and pale-chestnut bird with black crown

WV

PLUMAGE Black head (duller in winter, speckled); **yellow collar, underbody**; pale chestnut-brown mantle, feathers edged paler; **rufous rump. Female:** Dull-brown above, streaked; pale-buff below.

HABITS Normally gregarious; sometimes small bands with other birds; feeds on mud roads, fields. **Call:** Occ a *tzeet*.

RELATED RED-HEADED BUNTING *E bruniceps* **Rufous-chestnut crown, throat** (paler in winter); **yellower rump**; sighted Kalyan, Uran. Uncommon.

Uran
Karjat
Panvel
Wada
Murbad
Vadhkal
Malvani
occ Aarey, Talzan
Fairly common

CRESTED BUNTING *Melophus lathami*

6"

Crested, glossy black and chestnut bird. Sexes differ

R/LM

PLUMAGE Glossy black overall (has blue-black sheen); **deep-chestnut wings, tail; diagnostic** pointed, jet-black crest. **Female:** Pale olive-brown above, streaked; shorter, brown crest; **paler rufous-chestnut on wings, tail**; streaked breast.

HABITS Stony, grassy hill-slopes, often along roadsides; pairs or small bands with Tree Pipits, other buntings. **Call:** Soft *tsip* or quick *csink*, often several times; brdg males (early-Apr-Jul) have distinctive pleasant song.

Malshej Ghat
occ Karjat,
Matheran Range
also Naneghat,
Mblswr
Uncommon

URBAN AREAS

Parks, gardens, homes, industrial sheds, garbage dumps, landfill sites etc. The birds featured in this section comprise species that thrive in the vicinity of human activity in urban Mumbai.

BLACK KITE *Milvus migrans*

Common

PLUMAGE Dark-brown overall, with slight rufous tinge; **OH flight**, brown underbody, **diagnostic forked tail, pale patches on underwings.** Juv: Paler; streaked plumage.

HABITS Familiar, abundant raptor; large gatherings on landfill sites; largely scavenges; many roost together in large trees. Call: A long-drawn, whistling scream; most vocal Sep-Mar.

RELATED BLACK-EARED KITE *M m lineatus* **WV** slightly larger; in OH flight, more conspicuous white patch on underwings. Uncommon.

HOUSE SWIFT *Apus affinis*

6"

Small, dark swift, usually amid habitation

R

Common

PLUMAGE Deep-brown overall; **diagnostic white rump, throat**; short tail, very slightly forked, often indistinct; **in OH flight, white throat,** dark underbody, very slightly forked, fanned tail.

HABITS Common swift amid habitation; gregarious; often in crowded areas; short glide follows rapid wing-beats; may fly high. Call: Distinctive trilling calls, in flight and around roost/nesting site.

BARN OWL *Tyto alba*

14"

Golden-buff and white owl with striking face

R

 Common

PLUMAGE Pale golden-buff and grey above; finely-speckled black and white; **diagnostic white heart-shaped facial disc;** white below, faintly-speckled. **Blackish eyes.**

HABITS Urban Mumbai's common owl, found even in crowded localities; scattered family parties, pairs or solitary birds; rests during day in dark loft, shaded corners of buildings, amid overgrown vines, industrial sheds; emerges at dusk; rodents constitute major food. **Call:** Long-drawn *khheee* screech; various shrieking call-notes.

SPOTTED OWLET *Athene brama*

8"

Small, profusely-spotted, brown and white owl

R

Fairly common

PLUMAGE Sooty earthy-brown above, **spotted white;** pale-whitish nuchal collar, **facial-discs; bright-yellow eyes;** white chin, throat; pale below, marked darker. Juv: Streaked dark-brown breast, abdomen.

HABITS Spends day in tree-cavities, foliage or under house roofs; emerges around dusk; solitary or pairs; hawks insects around roadside lights at night. **Call: Diagnostic noisy** assortment of chattering, chuckling calls, mostly around dusk.

ALEXANDRINE PARAKEET *Psittacula eupatria*

21"

Long-tailed
green bird with
maroon-red
wing-patch

R

● ● ♪

Uncommon

*Occ S&C Mumbai.
Commoner over
N Mumbai*

PLUMAGE Grass-green overall; **rose-pink collar;
black stripe from chin/throat merges into pink
collar; diagnostic maroon-red wing-patch;**
heavy, hooked reddish beak. **Female:** Lacks pink
collar and black chin stripe. **Juv:** Like female.

HABITS Pairs or small bands; occ with
commoner Rose-ringed. **Call:** **Diagnostic** loud,
shrill *khrreaak* scream; calls mostly in flight.

ROSE-RINGED PARAKEET *Psittacula krameri*

17"

Noisy, long-tailed,
grass-green bird

R

● ● ♪

Common

PLUMAGE Bright grass-green overall; **rose-pink
collar; black chin stripe;** smaller size, absence of
maroon-red wing-patch, more gregarious nature
than Alexandrine. **Female:** Lacks pink collar and
black stripe.

HABITS Usually gregarious and noisy; favourite
feed and roost sites; raids fruiting orchards,
cultivation. **Call:** Shrill *kee-ak* or *kkreeak* scream;
distinctly less coarse than Alexandrine's; calls
frequently in flight.

ASIAN KOEL *Eudynamys scolopacea*

17"

Long-tailed, arboreal bird. Sexes differ

R

♪ ● ● ●

Fairly common

PLUMAGE Glossy-black overall; conspicuous **greenish beak; deep-crimson eyes.** Female: **Dark-brown above,** incl wings, tail; **profusely-stippled, barred white;** whitish below, spotted on foreparts, barred below breast.

HABITS Chiefly arboreal, commonly in crowded localities, dashing over city lanes; often in pairs; regularly visits fruiting/flowering trees; noisiest in summer; brood-parasitic on House Crow. Call: **Diagnostic;** male song a loud, whistling *kuoo-kuoo,* in crescendo; female has bubbling chatter, mostly in flight.

ROCK PIGEON *Columba livia*

13"

Well-known, blue-grey bird amid habitation

R

♪ ●

Common

PLUMAGE Blue-grey overall, with metallic-purple, green and reddish-purple sheen around neck, breast; **2 dark wing-bars,** conspicuous at rest and in flight.

HABITS Abundant, usually gregarious; great nos in every locality; commonest bird within Mumbai municipal limits; less common away from habitation, around cliffs. Call: Distinctive, deep, somewhat rolling *gooturr-goo;* also a nasal *gooo-goo-goo.*

HOUSE CROW *Corvus splendens*

PLUMAGE Blackish overall, with slight gloss; **pale ash-grey neck, nape and breast**, appearing as broad, contrasting collar; black beak, legs.

17"
Familiar blackish bird amid habitation
R

● ● ● ♪

Common

HABITS Abundant amid habitation; complete parasite on human world; highly adaptable, vigilant, plucky and quick; always discovering new nesting sites, feeding strategies; mostly scavenges; great gatherings at landfill sites; also visits fruiting, flowering trees. **Call:** Diagnostic; high-pitched *caaw* or *kwah*, slightly rasping in tone; occ a less shrill *kowk* and a pleasant *kurrrr*.

RELATED LARGE-BILLED CROW *Corvus macrorhynchos* **20-22"** Glossy-black overall, without contrasting grey; heavy-looking beak; less common, much more wary but less adaptable than the abundant House Crow; solitary or pairs, occ few together; less common amid habitation. Grating, deep *khaa* and *kraa* calls; occ a rapid gurgling note. Fairly common.

There are an estimated half-million House Crows in Mumbai. There is much concern that the rising crow numbers could be adversely affecting the populations of numerous smaller birds.

HOUSE SPARROW *Passer domesticus*

6"

Familiar bird around humans. Sexes differ

R

 Common

Quite unbelievably, there has been a marked decline in nos since the early-1990s; only a slight recovery observed in recent times

PLUMAGE Grey, chestnut, white and black head and **face**; rufous-chestnut mantle, streaked blackish; **white shoulder-patch; black centre of throat, breast**; dull-whitish below. **Female:** Pale ashy-brown above, profusely-streaked; lacks black below.

HABITS Familiar amid habitation; often gregarious, especially when roosting; scavenges, raids standing crop, grain shops; also feeds on insects when brdg (intermittently round the year with brief pause during monsoon). **Call:** Highly vocal; diagnostic, mix of chirps and soft screams.

COMMON MYNA *Acridotheres tristis*

10"

Familiar, brown bird with blackish head

R

Common

PLUMAGE Dark-brown above, with blackish head; **bright-yellow beak, legs and skin around eyes**; dull-brown below breast, whiter on lower abdomen, undertail-coverts; **striking white wing-patch**, best seen in flight; dark tail, tipped white on outer feathers.

HABITS Well-known bird amid habitation; usually several around; upright stance; alert, inquisitive, omnivorous; often around grazing cattle; visits flowering trees. **Call:** Diagnostic raucous jumble of chuckles, whistles and screams.

COPPERSMITH BARBET *Megalaima haemacephala*

6"

Chubby, green, yellow and crimson bird

R

Common

PLUMAGE Dark or olive-green above; **bright-crimson forehead**; yellow around eyes; **yellow throat**; **diagnostic bright-crimson breast patch**, dull-yellow below breast, broadly-streaked greenish; coral-red legs.

HABITS Arboreal; commonly heard, infrequently sighted; solitary or pairs; has benefited from the planting of fruiting, flowering and soft-wooded trees (Gulmohur, Copper Pod, Indian Coral, Pipal, Banyan). **Call: Diagnostic**; monotonous *took-took* or *tuk-tuk*, with a mellow, slightly-ringing quality; often ventriloquial; most vocal Dec-May.

ORIENTAL MAGPIE ROBIN *Copsychus saularis*

8"

Long-tailed, black and white bird. Sexes differ

R

Common

PLUMAGE Silky-blue wash to black head, neck, breast, mantle and wings; **black and white wings, tail**; white below breast. **Female: Duller** slaty-grey and white.

HABITS Usually pairs; family parties Jul-Oct; hops on ground, tail often cocked; visits flowering trees. **Call:** Plaintive *sweee*; sharp, whistling *schwee-cheche* before roosting; excellent songster, **diagnostic, rambling song of male** (Mar-Jul) from exposed perches; snatches of song occ round the year; also harsh, grating calls.

WHITE-THROATED FANTAIL *Rhipidura albicollis*

7"

Slaty-brown
bird with
often-fanned,
longish tail

R

Common

PLUMAGE Plain, slaty-brown above; white
supercilium; **diagnostic white chin, throat;
white-spotted, ashy-brown band across breast;**
white tips to all except central tail-feathers.

HABITS Often in mangrove creeks; restless,
fans tail often; often in mixed bird parties
Call: Diagnostic; rambling whistle of 5-7 notes,
quite human in quality; occ harsh alarm-notes.

RELATED **WHITE-BROWED FANTAIL** *R aureola*
Blackish throat; broad white supercilium, white-
spotted wing-bars. Uncommon. *See inset*

EURASIAN GOLDEN ORIOLE *Oriolus oriolus*

10"

Yellow and
black bird.
Sexes differ

R/WV

Fairly common

PLUMAGE Vivid golden-yellow overall; broad,
black eye-stripe; black wings, central tail-feathers.
Female: Pale yellow-green above; dull-white
below, streaked brown. Pinkish-red beak.

HABITS Strictly arboreal; usually pairs; occ small
bands in winter; with other birds on fruiting,
flowering trees. Call: An intermittent, fluty
pfee-loulo; also a harsh, grating *kheeha*, often as
an alarm-note.

COMMON TAILORBIRD *Orthotomus sutorius*

5"

Long-tailed, greenish bird with rufous crown

R

Common

PLUMAGE **Rusty-rufous crown** contrasts with **bright olive-green mantle, wings**; dull buff-white below. **Brdg Male**: **Pointed central tail-feathers**, up to 2" longer; small, dark patch on neck-sides (best seen when male calling on exposed perch).

HABITS Keeps to low vegetation, even potted plants; clambers up into trees; commonly breeds in large leaves of Indian Almond Tree; often heard but little seen. Call: Diagnostic, most vocal Apr-Sep; loud, *chwit-chwit* or *tuwit-tuwit*; brdg male may call 2-3 minutes at a stretch.

PURPLE-RUMPED SUNBIRD *Nectarinia zeylonica*

4"

Tiny, restless bird with yellow on underbody. Sexes differ

R

Common

PLUMAGE Striking **metallic-green crown, shoulder-patch; chestnut-maroon mantle; diagnostic** metallic-purple rump, chin, throat; **maroon band across upper-breast; lemon-yellow below**. **Female**: Ashy-brown above; **dull-white throat** contrasts with pale-yellow breast, belly.

HABITS Restless bird of foliage; regularly visits flowering plants, occ on high-rise buildings; pairs often close by. Call: A faint, chirping *tsesiwee*; brdg male (Feb-Apr, Jun-Oct) has sharp, twittering song, weaker than Purple Sunbird's.

RELATED & UNUSUAL SIGHTINGS

The list below is of Winter Visitors or Passing Migrants sighted by birdwatchers in the region or reported in various publications; for many of these species there have been sporadic sightings in the region during the past 25 years.

DARTER *Anhinga melanogaster* **33-36"** Sighted Powai, Vaitarna, Uran

GREYLAG GOOSE *Anser anser* **30 - 34"** 3 birds over Manori Creek

TUFTED DUCK *Aythya fuligula* **17-19"** Reported Vihar (SGNP), Vaitarna Lakes

MALLARD *Anas platyrhynchos* **21-24"** Reported NW Mumbai

LITTLE BITTERN *Ixobrychus minutus* **14"** Once in winter, S Mumbai

BLACK BITTERN *Dupetor flavicollis* **22-23"** Sighted Nhava (Uran area), Vihar Lake

GREY-HEADED FISH EAGLE *Icthyophaga ichthyaetus* **28"** Sighted Vihar, Tansa, Andhra (Lonavala) *Below*

PALLAS'S FISH EAGLE *Halieetus lencoryphus* **32"** Reported Tansa

LESSER ADJUTANT *Leptoptilos javanicus* **40-44"** Sighted Vihar Lake, 2001

LESSER FRIGATEBIRD *Fregata ariel* **28-30"** Occ during monsoon storms; sighted S Mumbai, Madh, Alibaug

GREAT FRIGATEBIRD *Fregata minor* **32-36"** Sighted S Mumbai coast

MASKED BOOBY *Sula dactylatra* **32-36"** S Mumbai, Gorai, Uttan, Kihim; mostly during monsoon storms

RED-FOOTED BOOBY *Sula sula* **26-30"** Reported S Mumbai, Aug 2001

INDIAN SKIMMER *Rynchops albicollis* **16"** Sighted Malshej plateau, Lonavala, Poladpur (Vashist River)

CRAB-PLOVER *Dromas ardeola* **16"** Sighted Gorai, Kelve, Kihim, Murud

GREAT THICK-KNEE *Esacus recurvirostris* **20"** Sighted Manor-Wada, Gorai, Panvel; reported Poladpur-Mahad

RED-NECKED PHALAROPE *Phalaropus lobatus* **7"** Reported Uran, Oct 2001

ORIENTAL PRATINCOLE *Glareola maldivarum* **10"** Sighted Charkop area, eastern side of Malad Creek, 1985

SMALL PRATINCOLE *Glareola lactea* **7"** Sighted Uran, Datiwere

BROAD-BILLED SANDPIPER *Limicola falcinellus* **7"** Sighted Uran; reported Thane Creek; could be commoner but overlooked

GREAT KNOT *Calidris tenuirostris* **11"** Sighted Uran; reported Rewas

SPOTTED REDSHANK *Tringa erythropus* **12"** Sighted Uran, Naigon/Bassein, Sewri Bay, Alibaug coast

INDIAN RIVER TERN *Sterna aurantia* **15–18"** Sighted Nirmal, Tansa, Uran, Roha, Poladpur

ROSEATE TERN *Sterna dougallii* **15"** Reported south of Alibaug

COMMON TERN *Sterna hirundo* **13"** Sighted Gorai, Manori, Murud; reported Alibaug

WHITE-CHEEKED TERN *Sterna repressa* **13"** Sighted/reported Uran, Murud, S Mumbai

LESSER-CRESTED TERN *Sterna bengalensis* **14"** Sighted

Alibaug-Rewas, Murud

WHITE-WINGED TERN Chlidonias leucopterus 9" Reported NW Mumbai coast, Uran

SOOTY TERN Sterna fuscata 14" Reported south of Mumbai

WHITE-TAILED LAPWING Vanellus leucurus 11" Sighted Uran, Manor

SPOTTED CRAKE Porzana porzana 9" Sighted MB marshes; reported Kalyan, Powai, Wada

EURASIAN SPARROWHAWK Accipiter nisus 12-14" Sighted Elephanta, Tansa, Matheran

BESRA Accipiter virgatus 12-14" Seen NW Mumbai, SGNP, Phansad

BONELLI'S EAGLE Hieraaetus fasciatus 26-28" Reported Bhmshnkr, Rajmachi area, Harishchandragadh

RED-HEADED VULTURE Sarcogyps calvus 33" Sighted Mumbra, Bhiwandi, Murud, Phansad

RED-NECKED FALCON Falco chicquera 12-14" Sighted Karjat, Wada

AMUR FALCON Falco amurensis 12" One sighting in SGNP

LONG-LEGGED BUZZARD Buteo rufinus 24" Sighted Elephanta, Yeur, Aarey

EGYPTIAN VULTURE Neophron percnopterus 24-26" Formerly bred Mumbra Hills; sighted Gorai, Khopoli-Pali Rd, Roha

PIED HARRIER Circus melanoleucos 17-19" Sighted along Malad Creek, Mira-Bhayandar marshes, off NH8 nr Shahpur; reported Dombvili, Diva

MONTAGU'S HARRIER Circus pygargus 18" Sighted Navi Mumbai, Karjat-Badlapur Rd, Murbad, Alibaug, Deccan

GREY FRANCOLIN Francolinus pondicerianus 13" Heard/ sighted Palghar-Datiwere-Kelve; widespread Deccan

BLUE-BREASTED QUAIL Coturnix chinensis 6" Sighted Aarey, Murbad, Dombivli; 1 caught on Malshej plateau in early-monsoon

LESSER YELLOWNAPE Picus chlorolophus 11" Sighted Mblswr; possibly Bhmshnkr

NILGIRI WOOD PIGEON Columba elphinstonii 16" Sighted Bhmskr, Phansad, below Mblswr; reported Matheran, SGNP Below

EURASIAN COLLARED DOVE Streptopelia decaocto 12-13" Seen Uran, Nagothane, Uttan, Ambernath

MALABAR GREY HORNBILL Ocyceros griseus 18" Sighted KBS, Bhmshnkr, Phansad

GREAT HORNBILL Buceros bicornis 40-44" Seen thrice Feb 2000 SGNP; may still exist in Shyd valleys

SAVANNA NIGHTJAR Caprimulgus affinis 9" Sighted SGNP, Malshej Ghat

WHITE-RUMPED NEEDLETAIL Zoonavena sylvatica 5" 2 sightings of fairly good-sized flocks over SGNP (2001); over forest

FORK-TAILED SWIFT Apus pacificus 7" A flock once over SGNP/ Aarey

RED-BREASTED PARAKEET
Psittacula alexandri 15"
Originally in Himalayan
foothills; few birds escaped
from captivity in the
mid-1990s and settled locally;
no confirmed brdg yet;
sighted several suburban
areas

COLLARED KINGFISHER
Todiramphus chloris 10"
Sighted Gorai, Manori Creek,
Elephanta

EUROPEAN ROLLER *Coracias
garrulus* 12" Sighted Karjat,
NW Mumbai, Mira-Bhayandar,

SIRKEER MALKOHA
Phaenicophaeus leschenaultii
17" Reported Murbad,
Ambernath-Badlapur

CHESTNUT-WINGED CUCKOO
Clamator coromandus 18"
Specimen found at Sion (1997)

SOUTHERN GREY SHRIKE *Lanius
meridionalis* 10" Reported Pen,
Wadkhal, Nagothane, Khodala

BLACK-NAPED ORIOLE *Oriolus
chinensis* 11" Sighted SGNP,
KBS, Phansad

ASIAN FAIRY BLUEBIRD *Irena
puella* 10" Once below
Mblswr; reported Phansad,
Bhmshnkr

BANK MYNA *Acridotheres
ginginianus* 9" Sighted around
cattle-shed off Western
Express Highway; reported
Panvel

ULTRAMARINE FLYCATCHER
Ficedula superciliaris 5" Twice
sighted SGNP (along Pongam
slope and near Culvert 14)

RUSTY-TAILED FLYCATCHER
Muscicapa ruficauda 6"

Reported SGNP, Phansad

LARGE GREY BABBLER *Turdoides
malcolmi* 11" Sighted Malshej
Ghat, Naneghat, Lonavala

ORPHEAN WARBLER *Sylvia
hortensis* 6" Sighted Aarey,
Manor, Gorai. *Below*

LESSER WHITETHROAT *Sylvia
curruca* 5" Most sites

PADDYFIELD WARBLER
Acrocephalus agricola 5"
Sighted MB marshes, Uran

TYTLER'S LEAF WARBLER
Phylloscopus tytleri 4" Sighted
Mblswr, SGNP, Tungareshwar,
Bhmshnkr

JUNGLE PRINIA *Prinia sylvatica* 5"
Reported Khopoli-Pali Rd,
Dombivli

ISABELLINE WHEATEAR *Oenanthe
isabellina* 7" Sighted Aksa,
Datiwere

TAWNY PIPIT *Anthus campestris* 6"
Sighted Uran, Kelve

BLYTH'S PIPIT *Anthus godlewskii* 7"
Reported Uran, Dombivli

GREY-NECKED BUNTING *Emberiza
buchanani* 6" Sighted Andheri,
Kalyan-Dombivli

OLD SIGHTINGS

These are some pre-1976 sightings from the Mumbai region.

Persian Shearwater, Wilson's
Storm Petrel, Fulvous Whistling
Duck, Common Shelduck
Greater Scaup, Common
Merganser, Water Rail, Little
Crake, Swinhoe's Snipe, Wood
Snipe, Eurasian Woodcock,
Sociable Lapwing, Pomarine
Skua, Parasitic Jaeger (Skua),
Sooty Gull, White-cheeked Tern,
Saunder's Tern, Bridled Tern,
Pallid Scops Owl, Eurasian
Nightjar, Sykes Nightjar, Sand
Martin, Plain Martin, Common
Starling, Southern Hill Myna,
Ashy Minivet, Richard's Pipit

FAR AFIELD

The following four species were sighted here between the late-1800s and early-1900s, far beyond their known ranges.

Note not just the species names but the locations where they were seen (reported in *The Birds of Bombay and Salsette* by Salim Ali and Humayun Abdulali, 1941)

DEMOISELLE CRANE
Several seen in Mumbai during the winter of 1900.

LESSER FLORICAN
Several records between 1889 and 1913 at Mahalaxmi, Catholic Gymkhana grounds on Kennedy sea face, sites between Malad and Andheri, Kalyan, between Alibag and Mandwa, Karjat and near Neral.

One of these sightings was near Churchgate Railway Station on 8 June 1913.

RED JUNGLEFOWL
Sighted by C McCann on hills behind Kanheri Caves, Borivli on 24 February 1929.

SARUS CRANE
Several seen in and around Mumbai during the winter of 1900; a solitary bird seen by HS Symons at Santacruz on 9 December 1908. A few days prior to this sighting he had seen a dead Sarus near Bandra railway station. He had also seen this species at Panvel in 1897 (a famine year upcountry).

The appearance of the Sarus in the Mumbai region has been linked to severe droughts during those years in Gujarat and the Deccan.

POWER PERCHES

Over the years, at least 62 species of birds have been observed perched on powerlines and transmission towers that criss-cross the length and breadth of this largely populous region.

With birds using powerlines and transmission towers as look-out perches for launching hunting sorties, resting, night roosting, advertising territory, or for feeding, these spots are a birdwatcher's delight.

COMMONLY SEEN
The most commonly-seen birds on overhead powerlines are Black Drongo, Green Bee-Eater, Long-Tailed Shrike, White-Throated Kingfisher, Barn and Red-Rumped Swallows.

Amongst raptors, Common Kestrel, Black-Shouldred Kite and Laggar Falcon have been regularly sighted on transmission towers and powerlines.

NESTING
The following species have been observed nesting on powerlines and transmission towers:
Black Kite, House Crow, Baya Weaver, Common Myna, Pied Myna.

On one occasion, a Purple Sunbird pair was observed building a nest on a transmission cable near the western border of SGNP.

DECAPITATED SPECIMENS
Decapitated specimens of the following species have also been seen (possibly the result of flying into powerlines):

Black Kite, Common Kestrel, Barn Owl, Grey Nightjar, Purple Heron, Pond Heron, Black-Crowned Night Heron, Wire-Tailed Swallow, White-Breasted Waterhen, Purple Swamphen, Slaty-Breasted Rail, Koel (male), Spotted Dove, Black Drongo.

HERONRIES IN THE REGION *Active during 1997-2002*

Most of these sites are active during the breeding season between mid-April and September.

Airoli (Siemens Compound); **Andheri W** (vicinity of Bhavan's College); **Bandra E** (several in Kala Nagar, MIG Clny); **Borivli W** (Gorai Rd; off SVP Road; Nr Bhagwati Hospital); **Byculla** Zoo (Veermata Jijabai Bhonsle Udyan); **Dadar** Parsee Colony; **Goregaon W** (Bangur Nagar; Excel Industries, off SV Road); **Kalyan-Badalapur**; **Kandivli W** (off MG Road); **Kanjurmarg** (off LBS Marg); **Kopar Khairane** (Dhirubhai Ambani Knowledge City, off Thane-Belapur Rd); **Malad** (Malavni area; Nr Link Road, Marve Road Jn); **Malad Creek** (nr Dharivali Tekdi); **Mira-Bhayandar** area (several sites);

Mulund (off LBS Marg); **Nhava** village area; **Pawane** (MIDC); Western side of **Powai** (Larsen and Toubro; IIT Campus – last seen 1998); **Uran 1** (behind TS Chanakya); **Vikhroli** (Godrej, Pirojshanagar – at least six sites, including in mangrove area); **Yari Road** (7 Bungalows – several sites).

BAYA COLONIES *Active during 1998-2002*

A species seriously affected by habitat loss in the urban areas; colonies come alive during monsoon (late-May-Sep). Majority of colonies are on Palmyras; some on Date Palms, Babuls, Su-babuls and Indian Jujubes.

Aarey (several scattered), **Aksa-Marve-Manori-Gorai** (several, scattered), **Alibaug-Mandwa Road, Alibaug-Revdanda Rd, Charkop/Talzan, Esselworld** (at least two large colonies), **Kandivli East** (Akurli Road), **Navi Mumbai, Pen,** Several along **Uran** (several small, scattered colonies), Very low-built nest colonies along **Mumbai-Pune**

Expressway, Vikhroli, Wadkhal-Poynad Road

IN OUR BACKYARD

Of the slightly over 300 bird species recorded so far in the metropolitan area and immediate neighbourhood, more than 150 have been sighted (regularly or sporadically) in city parks, gardens, on roadside trees, transmission towers and coastal fronts (creeks, beaches), despite the noise, stench and pollution! Most of these species are in small numbers and only the hardiest manage to survive in abundance. Indeed, their numbers have plummeted over the past decade.

Interestingly, Mumbai also has the unique distinction of having, besides coastal tracts, two amazingly contrasting worlds – the overbuilt city with its traffic jams and crammed garbage-laden lanes juxtaposed, mere minutes away, by a peerless National Park, a verdant, hilly realm of tropical forest and lakes.

Species of the following bird families have clearly divided themselves between Mumbai city (the city slickers) and the forest (wilder cousins). Several of the species listed exist in both habitats.

CITY SLICKERS	WILDER COUSINS
Red-vented Bulbul	Red-whiskered Bulbul
Tailor Bird, Ashy Prinia	Grey-breasted Prinia
Purple-rumped Sunbird	Purple Sunbird, Crimson Sunbird
Cattle Egret	Other egrets on lake-edges
Black Kite	Brahminy Kite on the lakes
Magpie Robin	Several thrushes
Blue Rock Pigeon	Green Pigeon, Emerald Dove
Alexandrine, Rose-ringed Parakeet	Plum-headed Parakeet
Red-breasted Parakeet (recent)	Blue-winged Parakeet (recent)
Koel	Several other cuckoos
House Crow	Jungle (Large-billed) Crow
Spotted Owlet	Jungle Owlet
Barn Owl	Brown Hawk Owl, Brown Fish Owl
Coppersmith (Crimson-breasted Barbet)	Brown-headed Barbet
Golden Oriole	Black-hooded Oriole
House Sparrow	Yellow-throated Sparrow
Black Drongo	Ashy (wintering) and several other drongos

ESCAPED CAGE-BIRDS
Escaped cage-birds that have been sighted here in recent times: Red-breasted parakeet (at least five locations in suburban areas); Grackle or Indian Hill Myna (once each in SGNP, Karnala).

Escaped cage-birds that have become established here: Pied starling, Alexandrine parakeet.

NOCTURNAL BIRDS
At least eight species of owls, four of Nightjars, Night Heron,

Lesser Whistling Teal, Painted Snipe and other snipes (winter), various rails, including Moorhen, waterfowl (chiefly winter), Little Green Heron – all on freshwater bodies. Several of these are crepuscular. Waders on tidal creeks; many waders are active on full-moon nights. Several of our wintering waterfowl feed during the night.

Several cuckoos (vocal mostly May-early-Sep). The diurnal Red-wattled Lapwing calls during the night, especially when disturbed.

PHOTO CREDITS *Photographs from PORPOISE PhotoStock*

NAYAN KHANOLKAR 2, 9
KRUPAKAR-SENANI 8
SUNJOY MONGA 1, 4-5, 6, 7, 15,

22, 72, 116, 154, 168 *bottom*
V MUTHURAMAN 168 *top*

ABBREVIATIONS

Bhmshnkr	Bhimashankar	lk	lake
brdg	breeding	LK	Lonavala-Khandala
crk	creek	Mblswar	Mahabaleshwar
incl	including	nr	near
jn	junction	occ	occasionally

ACKNOWLEDGEMENTS

Birds of Mumbai has been made possible thanks to the gracious support of Pan India Paryatan Limited (PIPL), promoters of Esselworld and Water Kingdom. The positive action of progressive corporates needs to be appreciated and I am sure many others will emulate PIPL and encourage such dovetailing of corporate and enviromental endeavours.

At PIPL, I am grateful to Mr Ashok Goel, Director, Esselworld & Water Kingdom, Mr Nilesh Mistry, Vice-President, Corporate Affairs, and Ms Prajakta Malgi, Asst. Manager, Corporate Communications, for their wholehearted support and enthusiasm.

I wish to also acknowledge the great contribution to the region and its many birdwatchers by the late Mr Humayun Abdulali, the bona fide birdwatcher extraordinaire.

The watercolour illustrations, vividly executed in meticulous detail by Carl D'Silva will be enjoyed by all. Thanks buddy for putting your heart into this project and thanks Barbara, for all your help and for tolerating Carl's long stay away from Goa. Special thanks to Anand Prasad for sharing many valuable notes on the region's ornithology, and to Deepak Chachra for doing the map.

There are many birdwatching colleagues with whom I have had great birding moments over the years. Joslin Rodrigues, SA Hussain, the late JS Serrao, Ulhas Rane, Dr Rene Borges, Kiran Srivastav, Vinod Haritwal, Digant Desai, Celine Anthony, Dr Salil Choksi, Aadesh Shivkar, Sanal Nair, Anil Pinto, Nitin Jamdar, Rishad Naoroji, Venkat Krishnan, Manisha Shah, Andrea Britto, Nivedita Kothare, Ashwini Vaidya, Sagar Mhatre, KB Singh, Vivek Kulkarni, Sunetro Ghosal, Vijay Avsare.

The Bombay Natural History Society has been a constant source of encouragement through its many programmes. I also thank officials of the Maharashtra State Forest Dept and of Jawaharlal Nehru Port Trust who have always been supportive.

And how can I ignore the many unidentified farmers, aunties and private estate owners whose fences and walls Joslin and I jumped over through the years to check some bird or a nest, always miraculously escaping being caught.

Thanks once again also to the India Book House team, to Padmini Mirchandani, Meera Ahuja, Gouri Dange, Priya Jhaveri and Jatin Lad.

The enthusiasm of Kathleen, Pamela and Capt Kevin Paul, the endless 'duckypond...' screams of little Yuhina and Kathleen whenever I would show them the birdlife on the little marshes around our home couldn't have been missed by those around.

I dedicate this guide to my many little friends, Yuhina, Akshita, Shivang, Simran, Mahima, Sujaan, Tej and Kathleen, and am sure their generation will produce some passionate birders with a special concern for the environment.

Finally, my deepest gratitude to my family, especially my mother and father, who encouraged my passion for birds at a time when it was considered a frivolous activity. My wife Jyoti's enthusiasm and support has always been a ray of hope.

SUNJOY MONGA
December, 2003

INDEX

COMMON NAMES

SCIENTIFIC NAMES